Editing Early Music

EARLY MUSIC SERIES

HOWARD MAYER BROWN
Embellishing Sixteenth Century Music

JAMES BLADES AND JEREMY MONTAGU
Early Percussion Instruments

JEREMY MONTAGU
Making Early Percussion Instruments

JAMES TYLER
The Early Guitar: A History and Handbook

LEOPOLD MOZART
A Treatise on the Fundamental Principles of Violin Playing
(Translated by Editha Knocker)

MICHAEL PRAETORIUS
Syntagma Musicum II: De Organographia 1 & 2
(Translated and Edited by David Z. Crookes)

JOHN CALDWELL

EDITING EARLY MUSIC

CLARENDON PRESS · OXFORD

Oxford University Press, Walton Street, Oxford OX2 6DP
London New York Toronto
Delhi Bombay Calcutta Madras Karachi
Petaling Jaya Singapore Hong Kong Tokyo
Nairobi Dar es Salaam Cape Town
Melbourne Auckland
and associated companies in
Beirut Berlin Ibadan Nicosia

Oxford is a trade mark of Oxford University Press

British Library Cataloguing in Publication Data
Caldwell, John, 1938
Editing early music.
1. Music printing
I. Title
686.28'4   ML112
ISBN 0-19-816143-3
ISBN 0-19-816142-5 Pbk

Library of Congress Cataloging in Publication Data
Caldwell, John, 1938—
Editing early music.
Bibliography: p. 114
Includes index.
1. Music—Editing.   I. Title.
ML63.C29   1984   781'.2   83-25056
ISBN 0-19-816143-3
ISBN 0-18-816142-5 (pbk.)

Set by Hope Services, Abingdon
Printed in Great Britain by
J. W. Arrowsmith Ltd, Bristol

Preface

This book has been prepared at the request of the publisher as a replacement for the similarly entitled pamphlet by Thurston Dart, Walter Emery, and Christopher Morris (Novello, OUP, and Stainer & Bell, 1963). Its aim, like that of its predecessor, is to offer advice about editorial procedures suitable for the music of earlier times. Because the expression 'early music' can cover such a wide chronological period, however, the material has been divided into three broad historical categories. The discussion of properly editorial matters has also been separated from advice on the preparation of printer's copy. At the same time there is no attempt to instruct in the detailed technicalities of palaeography, notation, and source studies. Those are the province of lengthier and more specialized works. It is intended rather for the guidance of those who have acquired a good knowledge of their chosen field, but who may not have thought very deeply about the problems of presentation in the form of an edition. Allusion is thus necessarily made to technical matters which are not here fully explained.

A great deal of 'early music' is still published today in editions which for one reason or another are inadequate. At one time it could be said that the main need was for editions of almost any sort, provided that they helped to fill the yawning chasms in the published repertory. I believe that the present need is for editions of the utmost integrity. The requirements of performers and scholars are—or should be—identical; the effort spent in satisfying them in the most economical way is richly rewarding. Even the best-intentioned editor can lapse, but the important thing is to learn from one's mistakes, and the present book is offered as the fruit of trial and error in the editing of various different kinds of music.

This publication has in a sense grown out of an occasional seminar on editing and transcribing to which postgraduate students at Oxford contributed by offering their own transcriptions for criticism, and by making searching evaluations of existing editorial endeavours within their field. I am grateful to these students, who have made me aware of so many problems which would otherwise have passed me by, and to the publishers for encouraging me to pursue the subject in book form. It would be invidious for the most part to name individual pupils, but Mr C. T. Johnson has been of particular help in supplying me with technical information about German keyboard tablatures, while Mr Matthew Spring has performed a similar service with regard to the lute repertory. I have also benefited greatly from discussions with Dr F. W. Sternfeld, Dr Susan Wollenberg, and Dr Roger Wibberley. Much insight has been provided by individual editors of the series *Musica da Camera*, with several of whom I have conducted a most interesting correspondence; the opportunity of editing this series has been invaluable. At a late stage Dr John Milsom and Mr Richard Abram read the complete typescript and made numerous helpful suggestions. Finally I thank my colleague Mr M. B. Parkes, Fellow of Keble College and University Lecturer in Palaeography, for his penetrating advice at all stages, and my wife for her proof-reading and constant affectionate encouragement. I am solely responsible for any errors, whether of fact or of judgement, that remain.

Oxford, 1984   John Caldwell

Note   English rather than US terminology is used for note-values, e.g. semibreve, quaver (not whole-note, eighth-note). This is also the basis of the abbreviations suggested in Appendix I, which US editors may wish to modify in consequence. 'Bar-line' = US 'bar'; 'bar' = US 'measure'.

Contents

List of Abbreviations

AcM	*Acta Musicologica*
CEKM	*Corpus of Early Keyboard Music* (American Institute of Musicology, 1963-)
CMM	*Corpus Mensurabilis Musicae* (American Institute of Musicology, 1947-)
CS	E. de Coussemaker, ed.: *Scriptorum de Musica Medii Aevi Nova Series a Gerbertina altera*, 4 vols. (Paris, 1864-76, and reprints)
CSM	*Corpus Scriptorum de Musica* (American Institute of Musicology, 1950-)
Cw	*Das Chorwerk*, ed. F. Blume and K. Gudewill (Berlin and Wolfenbüttel, 1929-)
DDT	*Denkmäler Deutscher Tonkunst*, 65 vols. (Berlin, 1892-1931, reprinted Wiesbaden and Graz, 1957-60)
DM	*Documenta Musicologica* (Kassel and Basel, 1955-)
EECM	*Early English Church Music* (London, 1963-)
GS	M. Gerbert, ed.: *Scriptores Ecclesiastici de Musica Sacra potissimum*, 3 vols. (Sankt-Blasien, 1784, and reprints)
JAMS	*Journal of the American Musicological Society*
MB	*Musica Britannica* (London, 1951-)
MC	*Musica da Camera*, ed. J. Caldwell (London, 1972-)
MD	*Musica Disciplina*
MGG	*Die Musik in Geschichte und Gegenwart*, ed. F. Blume, 16 vols. (Kassel and Basel, 1949-79)
ML	*Music and Letters*
MMMA	*Monumenta Monodica Medii Aevi*, ed. B. Stäblein (Kassel and Basel, 1956-)
MQ	*The Musical Quarterly*
MRM	*Monuments of Renaissance Music*, ed. E. Lowinsky (Chicago and London, 1964-)
NBA	J. S. Bach, *Neue Ausgabe Sämtlicher Werke* (Kassel and Basel, 1954-)
PMFC	*Polyphonic Music of the Fourteenth Century*, ed. L. Schrade and others (Monaco, 1956-)

PRMA	*Proceedings of the Royal Musical Association*
RISM	*Répertoire International des Sources Musicales* (Munich and Duisberg, 1960–)
RRMR	*Recent Researches in the Music of the Renaissance* (New Haven and Madison, 1964–)

List of Tables

List of Musical Examples

The author and publisher wish to thank Messrs. Bärenreiter-Verlag and Möseler Verlag for permission to reproduce examples 4 and 2.

I

Principles of Transcribing
and Editing

There are really only two fundamental requirements for an edition of music: clarity and consistency. In this respect there is no difference between a 'scholarly' and a 'practical' edition. The aim in both should be the same: to provide a musical text which can be trusted, and to do so in such a way that the music can be easily assimilated by the eye. There is no place for 'scholarly' editions which use barely legible forms of notation, or for 'practical' editions which provide insufficient information about the materials on which the text is based. Of course a sumptuously designed collected edition can often afford to include supplementary information—biographical, documentary, etc.—which is not strictly germane to the text; but that is another matter. The text of a collected edition should be performable as it stands. In the same way a 'practical' edition, however much advice it may give to the performer, should not distort the original and should be careful to distinguish between the composer's work and the editor's.

Editing is always more than mere transcription, although the latter is obviously a very important stage in the process. Strictly speaking a transcription is just a copy, but the advent of cheap and speedy photography has meant that many types of literal copying are no longer necessary. In the old days, scholars often made extremely close transcripts of ancient notation—'diplomatic'[1] transcriptions in the narrowest sense—as the basis of their editorial work. Sometimes these were even published. Nowadays such transcribing is rarely necessary, and in the case of more recent music, legibly notated in score, it may be possible to proceed directly to the preparation of the printer's copy. In some cases, indeed, a printer can be given a suitably annotated photograph of the original source, or of a previous edition if it

[1] Diplomatic: so-called because the science of exact transcription was first applied to historical documents of the type known as 'diplomas' (literally 'folded into two'). See J. Mabillon, *De re diplomatica* (Paris, 1681).

is no longer copyright (though such forms of time-saving have their hazards). But there remains a vast mass of music which for one reason or another requires a draft transcription as a bridge between the source and the final edition. The original may be written in obsolete notation, or it may require scoring, or both. Where the original notation is unambiguous, it may be systematically modernized at this stage. The important thing is to note down any factors which might conceivably affect the choice of reading: clefs, key-signatures, time-signatures, or mensuration signs, the placing of accidentals, line-ends, ligatures, coloration, and so on, depending to a certain extent on the date of the source. The initial transcription should be designed to accommodate variants from other sources, and to permit the ultimate use of a different source as the basis of the edition if that should prove desirable. If the sources are widely divergent, it may be necessary to make separate transcriptions directly from two or more of them.

Let us assume that the potential editor has mastered the techniques of transcription as they apply in his chosen field. The main editorial tasks are of course the assembling, transcription, and collation of the sources for the edition, and the choice of readings on which it will be based; but before these points can be considered it will be necessary to give some thought to the possible aims of a scholarly performing edition. An obvious prima facie answer would be simply: 'to reproduce the intentions of the composer'. Unfortunately that may often be a chimerical ideal. In earlier music, those intentions may simply not be ascertainable, owing to the lack of sources sufficiently close to the composer in time or cultural milieu, or to lack of precision in the notation of those which have come down to us. An acceptable substitute may be to reproduce a version which can be shown to have been current at some particular time and place. For such a purpose, the reproduction of a single representative source may be the best method. The objective value of such a procedure may in any case commend it as being preferable to a more fanciful solution; and it is a legitimate method in itself where the object is to illustrate a repertory or a scribal choice.

In many instances a composer may be seen to have revised his work, once or even several times; and sometimes he may never have committed himself to a definitive version. Handel, Beethoven, and in modern times Bruckner and Musorgsky are composers noted for their penchant for revision and in some cases indecision. A counsel of perfection would be to select a version approved by the composer at some stage and to stick to that. But for various reasons a conflation of various versions may be preferable in performance, and the editor will have to decide whether to attempt this as the basis of an edition (in which case the evidence for it will have to be fully recorded), or to print the separate versions *in extenso* and merely suggest a performing version. The types of evidence available for making editorial decisions will vary according to time, place, and genre: for a work by Dunstable the evidence may take the form of a number of manuscripts in differing relationships to the composer's intentions; for Byrd or Tallis the conflicting claims of manuscript sources and a printed edition might have to be considered; with Beethoven, the whole apparatus of manuscripts (autograph or copies), printed editions ('authentic' and otherwise), engraved plates, discarded proof sheets, subsequent alterations, sketch-books, letters, and conversation-books may have to be brought into play. If on the balance of probabilities the reader of this book is more likely to be concerned with composers of lesser stature, he will nevertheless find it instructive to study the critical reports of editors who have had to tackle such problems. The difficulties faced by editors of literature are also worthy of attention.[2]

The first task of any editor, therefore, is to assemble all the evidence relevant to the making of the edition and to ensure that none has been overlooked. Modern developments in bibliography have lessened the danger of omitting essential material, though in the last resort there is always an element of risk and even the most experienced editor can be caught out. Nor is it always possible to be certain how many copies of (say) an eighteenth-century printed edition it might be desirable to consult; close study can sometimes reveal variants (e.g. substituted or altered plates) in every extant copy. At the same time political factors, or difficulties of communication, may hinder the acquisition of material known to exist; and it may be practicable to consult certain copies only in microfilm or some other type of photographic reproduction (this is often perfectly safe, but can sometimes obscure important evidence obtainable only from the original).

[2] See Bibliography, 1(a).

If the source situation is complex, it may be possible, or indeed desirable, to eliminate whole classes of 'secondary' material throwing no light on the composer's intentions or the performing practice of his day. The editor should report the existence of such material and explain why it is not being used.

Having assembled his sources, the editor must assess their relative value, having regard to the aim of his edition as discussed above. There are no hard and fast rules for doing this. The solution may be perfectly obvious, if for example there is only a single source (even though it may itself be corrupt), or a primary source to which all others are clearly subsidiary. In more complex cases it is helpful to construct a stemma: a diagram illustrating the relationship, or the supposed relationship, between the sources (including lost sources whose existence can be inferred from the evidence). The comparison of variant readings can often demonstrate the probable relationship between two or more sources and their derivation from an 'archetype', the ancestor of all the surviving sources. If this is extant or can be reconstructed with confidence, its readings supplant those of its derivatives. But there may be insufficient evidence on which to make a reconstruction: there may be too few sources, and those but distantly related; it may be difficult, especially in music, to establish particular variants as erroneous and hence as evidence of descent from a more correct source; a scribe or printer may have made emendations on his own account, or selected his readings from more than one source ('contamination'). A newly discovered source may destroy the whole basis of an apparently correct stemma.[3]

In such cases it is preferable, rather than to attempt to reconstruct the archetype, to select a single source and to emend it where necessary. The evidence of other sources may still be helpful, but a haphazard conflation based on pragmatic or subjective criteria is to be avoided. Unless it has been chosen for

[3] For a good account of stemmatic method see Reynolds and Wilson, *Scribes and Scholars* (listed in the Bibliography, 1(a)); also the article 'Textual Criticism' in *The Oxford Classical Dictionary* (2nd edn., ed. N. G. L. Hammond and H. H. Scullard, Oxford, 1970). Philological considerations, which are the primary tool of stemmatics, do of course require adaptation in relation to music (though the parallels are certainly suggestive); and it is important to remember that all classes of evidence, some of which are likely to manifest themselves only to the close student of a particular repertory, are of value in establishing filiation. For a useful demonstration in a musical context see L. Hoffman-Erbrecht in E. Lowinsky, ed., *Josquin des Prez* (London, 1976), pp. 285-93.

the sake of its repertory and cultural significance, the primary source will be the one which, on balance, appears to preserve the best readings. But it may still be possible to infer in particular instances that a˙ subsidiary source is closer to the composer's intentions. In any event, whatever the editor's approach to textual criticism, the most objective method of presentation is likely to be that which takes a single source as its point of reference. The advice given in the following pages is largely based on this assumption, since even where the stemmatic method can be applied, the edition must show the evidence for the reconstruction. That is not to say, however, that an experienced editor handling complex materials may not vary the recommendations to suit the situation.

No editor should hesitate to emend rationally. But it should always be possible to explain how a corruption has arisen. The mistake may have occurred in the source being considered, or at a higher point in the 'family tree'. If an emendation proposed on such grounds can be shown to exist in another source, so much the better; but this will not automatically validate it, nor will its absence elsewhere automatically invalidate it. Situations vary so much that it is impossible to lay down strict rules. If there is an equal choice between emending and not emending, the editor should not emend. The maxim *difficilior lectio potior* may be borne in mind: it can sometimes happen that a scribe or printer has 'edited out' a technical or stylistic awkwardness rather than that the alternative reading is a corruption. But the only safe rule is to apply common sense; the better the editor knows his sources and his composer or repertoire, the more likely he is to arrive at the right answers.

It remains in this introductory chapter to discuss in general the ways in which editorial information may best be given. An introductory note of some kind is a *sine qua non* for an edition of early music; and a discussion of the source or sources is the irreducible minimum of information required. It is usual also to include some biography or historical background, but the extent of this will depend on the character of the edition or the conventions of a series, and on the nature of the material. There is little point in summarizing the life of a great composer who figures in standard works of reference: in such cases the immediate circumstances of the work's composition are a more valuable contribution. For older composers, biography in the exact sense may be unattainable; here too, historical background, with a discussion of such matters as liturgical or social context, is more appropriate.

'Discussion of sources' may range from the simple identification of a sole source to an elaborate assessment of a number of them. In any case, certain standards for citing sources should be maintained. For a printed edition, the information content of a catalogue entry in the British Library (as given in the *British Union-Catalogue of Early Music*) is an acceptable minimum. The typography of original title-pages may be retained to the extent of distinguishing between upper- and lower-case lettering, and between roman and italic type (line-ends would then be indicated by vertical strokes). Title-pages need not always be cited in full – they can be very lengthy – but the publisher's name, with the place and date (if given) of publication, is always included, separated if necessary from the title proper by a row of dots to indicate an omission. It is sometimes useful to add the format (in size, preferably in millimetres, or by such terms as octavo, quarto, folio), the number of pages, and the publisher's 'plate-mark' (his 'edition-number', so to speak). This can still leave some of a bibliographer's questions unanswered; but even at this level of information it is possible on occasion to reveal the existence of a hitherto unrecorded edition, issue, or 'state'.[4] One should always indicate which copy (or copies) one has used, and the shelf-mark (or 'press-mark') if it is from a public collection.

A manuscript should be cited by means of its location, the name of the library in which it is housed, and the shelf-mark in the form used in the library itself. Beware of obsolete shelf-marks: a letter to the librarian of a distant library may resolve a

---

[4] There is no agreed convention as to terminology. An 'issue' is, or ought to be, a single batch or printing for distribution to the booksellers. To constitute a second or subsequent 'edition', an issue should be from a different publisher, should incorporate substantive changes, or should be printed from newly engraved plates (or any combination of these). A new title-page by the same publisher does not of itself make an issue a new edition. A separate 'state' implies alteration to existing plates, or a mixture of plates engraved at different times, or both; but the evidence may not enable the examples of it to be identified as a specific 'edition' or 'issue'. What has been said of engraved plates applies of course *mutatis mutandis* to other processes such as type-setting. Modern bibliography has adopted slightly different definitions (see *The Oxford Dictionary for Writers and Editors* s.v. 'edition', 'impression', 'issue'), but these are not entirely relevant to the printing of music in earlier times.

doubtful instance. Manuscripts may be designated subsequently by sigla (abbreviated symbols); but it is essential to provide a key, even if they are those of an established bibliography such as the *Répertoire International des Sources Musicales* (*RISM*). But it is often better for editorial purposes to devise one's own sigla: a series of letters may suffice, if necessary printed in bold type for readier identification.

The identification and discussion of sources is often most usefully given as part of a preface or introduction, which will begin, perhaps, with more general information of a biographical and historical nature. It is of course perfectly possible to have a subsection on sources, with its own heading. Two distinguished scholarly series, *Musica Britannica* and *Early English Church Music*, in which an editor has often to consider a very large number of sources, have established the practice of listing them at the end, between the music and the critical commentary. This is often the neatest way, and it by no means precludes a more generalized discussion in the preface. Indeed, the editor of a large volume may initially be able to refer to his sources only in a very general way, partly because of their number and partly because their relative value may vary from one piece to another. In such a case, the notes on individual pieces will have to list the sources used and to indicate their relative significance.

Almost any edition of early music will need to include information on methods of performance. In most scholarly series this is given as a separate section. Its content may vary widely, and depends on what interpretative help is to be included in the score itself. It is now generally accepted that the score ought to be kept as clear as possible; this places the onus on the editor to provide sufficient information in his notes on performance. But circumstances vary: it may be impossible to convey in a preliminary note all the complexities of ornamentation or rhythmic alteration required. In such cases a subsidiary staff above the score may enable a solution to be given under the eye of the performer. The important thing, however, is that the notes and the score should match up intelligently. Some advice on the presentation of ornamentation, articulation, and rhythmic alteration in Baroque music will be given in Chapter 4. Other matters that an editor will have to consider include such things as instrumentation (or vocal scoring), pitch, and the general style of performance. Here it is important, while conveying the necessary historical information, not to be too dogmatic. It is one thing to point out the virtues of the Baroque flute (let us say) in the performance of Bach's flute sonatas, to describe its main technical features, and to indicate how its use affects the style of performance. But to imply that only a Baroque instrument can give a satisfactory result is not only to alienate users of an edition and reduce its sales (perhaps drastically); it is also to espouse a philosophy of absolute purism which rules out a great deal of effective re-creation of old music. An editor may most usefully suggest how a knowledge of old instruments (or of the constitution of choirs in former days) may be helpful in forming a correct style of performance.

All editions of old music require a statement of editorial method. This has an even more obviously direct relationship with the musical text as printed. On the whole, the older the music, the more will be the information that is needed. Specialized advice will be given in subsequent chapters of this book; all that need be said here is that, although certain conventions may be well established, they still need to be stated in the edition. It is particularly important to ensure that conventions regarding accidentals are fully explained and consistently carried out in the edition itself.

The final section of letterpress will be a critical commentary (as it is now generally called), a statement of departures from the source or sources, and of variants between them. Again, subsequent chapters of this book will contain more detailed advice, but one or two general points may be considered here. First, as to layout. There is no doubt that a generous layout, with a minimum of abbreviation and a clearly tabulated list of readings, is the ideal; but most publishers nowadays insist on a high degree of abbreviation and continuous rows of type. Study of the systems employed in the series *Musica Britannica*, *Early English Music*, and (for Baroque and Classical music) *Musica da Camera* will reveal the kinds of problems encountered and some possible solutions. One has only to compare these with the old collected editions of Bach, Josquin, Obrecht, or Ockeghem to see the advantages of the older methods.[5] But in these days the

---

[5] Some editors have used footnotes, which is in conformity with good literary usage. In large numbers they can create difficulties with the layout of the page; but it is possible to limit footnotes to variants of especial interest to the performer, relegating others to the commentary. Alternatively, one may draw attention to variants of particular interest by means of a special sign in the score.

need for economy is likely to be paramount; and compression need not necessarily mean incomprehensibility. Remember that the commentary is supposed to list variants *in terms of the score with which they are printed.* A logical order for each entry is: bar-number; staff; source (if necessary); description of variant readings (e.g. 23 III C 1st note *a'*). Alternatively, the readings of each source may be listed in turn; or the editor may give the readings of individual parts one by one. Each entry may be separated by a diagonal stroke to avoid columnation. The staff may be designated either by a (roman) numeral or by an abbreviated part-name.[6] I do not think it worth while to devise a numerical system for position within a bar: it is easier to say (for instance) '5th note' than to bother with superscript numerals, which in any case play havoc with the logical order of the entry. The first of the methods suggested enables the readings of more than one source to be incorporated within the same entry. In describing a variant, either use no verb or the present tense. (Avoid '5th note was *d*': it probably still is, if anyone cares to go and have a look. Use the past tense only for lost or destroyed sources.) The Helmholtz system is a universally accepted method of pitch nomenclature.[7] Refer to the note-values of your edition, not to those of the source if they are different.[8] Do not hesitate to describe more fully in words anything to which the accepted jargon is unequal.

Secondly, as to content. It is unrealistic to suppose that every single difference between a source and the edition, or between sources, can be shown. The important thing is to decide which classes of variant are to be noted, and to be consistent in doing so. It is sometimes possible to ignore whole categories, such as differences in ligatures, coloration, word-underlay, and so on, especially in late or otherwise untrustworthy sources. Much will depend on the 'aim of the edition' and the relationship between the sources. The selection of readings should of course illuminate all cases of emendation and adequately illustrate the editor's view of the sources as they relate to one another. The formula

---

6 See list of suggested abbreviations, Appendix II.

7 See Appendix I.

8 This rule may be reversed if there has to be frequent mention of obsolete technicalities, e.g. '*brevis* coloured in MS', where simply to give the consequential reading in terms of the transcription does not properly convey the nature of the error. But the commentary should be consistent throughout in this respect, and the method adopted made absolutely clear.

'obvious errors have been corrected' is not a very happy one. It is more honest to note every corrected error except, perhaps, the most trivial accidents of typography (a crotchet upside down, or without a stem, for instance).

Not all editorial material need be confined to the critical commentary. Modern convention rightly distinguishes between editorial and original accidentals, dynamics, and other such material in the score itself.[9] How this may best be done is discussed in the following pages. (A summary of the recommendations is given in Appendices I and IV.) Certain types of lacuna, as well as editorial suggestions for performance, may be given, small or in square brackets, without further remark. It is also possible to present a good deal of source information in preliminary staves placed before the score starts. (This is a valuable transcribing habit which might well be carried over into editions of many kinds of music.) To show original clefs in this way does not necessarily affect the user's assessment of editorial decisions; but it provides valuable information in a convenient form for the scholar, who may wish to draw deductions about scoring, pitch, and the like from the observation of such details; and in Baroque music a clef may provide good evidence for the choice of instrument. An original key-signature, which may very well have a bearing on the editor's interpretation of accidentals, is most conveniently shown in this form, even though subsequent changes may have to be consigned to the commentary. It is also helpful to show the ranges of parts (at least in medieval and Renaissance music); and if the preliminary staves contain nothing else, this is a good point at which to show it. But the preliminary staves may also show the first note or phrase in the original notation, in which case the ranges are better shown at the beginning of the score proper, in the context of modern clefs.

It is often desirable for an editor to indicate recommended

9 There is obviously a distinction to be drawn between the establishment of the text as such and its supplementation in order to realize the composer's or copyist's intentions as faithfully as possible in performance. Emendations and additions arising out of the former must be recorded in the commentary but do not in principle require typographical distinction; additions or changes in the latter category do so. But in practice, owing to the difficulty of tracing the literal form of a musical text beyond the extant sources, it is usually more convenient to regard all purely additional material (such as signs of mensuration and proportion, accidentals, dynamics, ornaments, and conjectural restorations) as 'editorial', and it is with this in mind that the term is used in this book.

tempos and tempo relationships between sections of a single movement. Editorial tempo markings, whether they are metronomic indications, verbal directions, or both, are simply placed in square brackets. (It is often obvious that they must be editorial, but there is an advantage in observing a uniform practice throughout the whole range of 'early music'.) Tempo relationships, however, need not be placed within square brackets, though they may be given round brackets (possibly with a footnote reference to fuller discussion in the commentary) if there is doubt as to their correctness. As with the indication of reduced time-values, they state an objective fact about the music which is nonetheless couched in a form which can only be editorial.

The logical order for indicating a tempo relationship is to state the value of the new section in terms of that of the old, e.g. $\textphrase$ = $\textphrase$ (of what preceded). In this case, the formula appears at the beginning of the new section of music, and is not ambiguous if correctly placed. The alternative is to use the following device:

$$\leftarrow \; \textphrase = \textphrase \; \rightarrow$$
$$\| \tfrac{6}{4}$$

in which the equals-sign appears directly above the double bar-line.[10] At the end of a line or page, there will usually be room (because of the occurrence of a new time-signature) to print the entire form there. Any original sign of mensuration or proportion should be given above the staff at the beginning of the new section, directly above the modern time-signature; it should be followed by an indication of the editorial scale of reduction if this has been changed or is at all ambiguous.[11]

Two or three further points of general application may be made here. In metrical music, the editor should normally introduce (or retain, or substitute) regular barring, both for help in interpretation and performance and for purposes of reference. Bars should normally be numbered from the left-hand ends of lines (except for the first), not counting any preliminary parts of a bar. The printer will transfer them to the beginning of his own lines if these are different (see also Chapter 5, footnote 2).

The late Thurston Dart's convention for an editorial tie or slur ⌒ is simple and generally applicable. The conventional

---

[10] If the placing is accurate, the arrows may be omitted, though the writer recommends their retention.

[11] Throughout this book, mensuration signs are given in bold type, modern time-signatures in ordinary face.

signs for ligatures and coloration, which are discussed at greater length in later chapters, are ⌐⎯⌐ and ⌐ ⌐ respectively.

In the presentation of text, care should be taken to distinguish between hyphens, used to separate syllables, and the continuous, ground-level line used to indicate the prolongation of the last syllable of a word. The latter conventionally extends to the last notational symbol of the phrase to which the syllable is being sung.[12] The extensive use of such lines in highly melismatic passages can lead to confusion with the lines of the staff, and in medieval and Renaissance music they might well be omitted altogether. Likewise, editorial slurs indicating syllable changes are unnecessary and confusing, and should not be used. Separate syllables, however, do in my opinion require separate (i.e. unbeamed) symbols, though this is clearly a matter on which views may differ. This and similar points are discussed more fully in subsequent chapters.

In what follows, the reader will detect a certain bias—if it is not already evident—towards forms of notation closer to the original than is sometimes favoured, towards a fuller rather than a more attenuated listing of sources and their variants, towards a plain rather than a heavily adorned text, wherever there is a legitimate choice of methods. The difficulty of certain archaic notations, the irrelevance of detailed commentary, and above all the unimaginative illiteracy of the present-day performer, seem to me to be often grossly exaggerated. Fortunately, the recent fashion for undue interference with what the composer wrote is rapidly passing. The editorial task is severe enough without making things harder than they need be. And the performer— amateur and professional—is becoming ever more sophisticated in his response to a wide and challenging variety of styles of the past.

---

[12] In older printing a row of dots is often used at the end of a word, but this could convey an erroneous impression that something has been omitted, and it has an inelegant appearance. When *Mensurstrich* is used (see below, p. 49), the word-end line is usually prolonged to the point at which the sound actually ceases, though precise usage varies from one publisher to another.

Medieval and Early Renaissance Music

This chapter deals with the period up to about 1450, though some of its recommendations are applicable to the early part of the following period as well.

Medieval music presents perhaps the severest problems to the editor. A legible transcription into modern notation necessarily results in an appearance totally at variance with that of the original source; and yet the editor must be sure to avoid anachronistic conventions. A further difficulty is that the transcription of a good deal of medieval music involves a certain amount of conjecture; but the editor must commit himself to the solution of problems which may not readily admit of one. We shall consider first some of the difficulties associated with the presentation of mensurable music, before going on to consider the special problems of monophony and some smaller points of detail.

Whatever one's prejudices and instincts may be, any attempt to match the note-values of the sources, especially in the earlier part of the period, would be wholly misplaced. Modern longs, breves, semibreves and minims do not even have the merit of looking like their forebears of the thirteenth and fourteenth centuries, and the numerous ligatures have no modern equivalent at all. Not even Wooldridge transcribed the music of Perotinus (*fl. c.* 1200) as literally as that. But Coussemaker and Wolf, amongst others, retained the 'original' values for some of their (now obsolete) transcriptions of music of the later thirteenth century, giving it a strangely Brobdignagian appearance. Wooldridge used minims and semibreves—reduction to a quarter of the original—in his transcription of Perotinus' 'Viderunt'; Husmann reduced this to one-eighth (six-four time), while still more recent editors —such as Apel, Waite, and Thurston—reduce to one-sixteenth. This last undoubtedly conveys the rhythmic idioms of this music best.

The historical tendency in the Middle Ages was for note-values to get smaller and smaller; and this necessitates corresponding changes in the scale of reduction in modern transcription. For music of the late thirteenth and early fourteenth centuries, a reduction to one-eighth is appropriate. I myself would retain this for music of the early Ars Nova at least, as it shows the rhythmic organization of this music so much more clearly; and it may be considered appropriate for even later works in an archaic rhythmic idiom, such as Machaut's *Messe de Nostre Dame*. But for most fourteenth-century music (except perhaps in England), and for that of the early fifteenth century, quartered values are suitable. During the course of the fifteenth century, halved values may be substituted; while from the sixteenth century onwards I would argue for original values in most cases (see Tables I–V, pp. 15, 16, 18–19, 20–21, 26).[1]

The question of time-values is complicated by the special character of Italian fourteenth-century music, and by the advent of the proportional system. For the most archaic Italian idioms, a breve:crotchet (or dotted crotchet) correspondence is appropriate; for more recent styles, the breve may be represented by the minim, dotted minim, or dotted minim tied to dotted crotchet, and smaller values accordingly. It is a peculiarity of Italian notation that a breve might contain four, six, eight, nine, or twelve|minims,[2] so that a single scale of reduction over the whole range of note-values is impossible. One might alternatively represent the minim by (say) a quaver and adjust the value of the breve accordingly; but this is less in accord with the historical basis of the notation.[3] In French notation, by contrast, the minim was uniform throughout the range of available metres.

The origins of the proportional system are uncertain, but its mathematical basis is straightforward: time-values under a proportional time-signature (which may take the form of a

---

[1] The recommendations of Apel (1953) are based partly on the exigencies of pedagogic method. He sometimes calls for greater reductions than considerations of legibility would seem to warrant.

[2] Originally known as *semibreves minimae*, these being the shortest 'semibreves' admissible in a particular mensuration.

[3] A comparison of the many modern editions of Italian fourteenth-century music will reveal the variety of approaches possible: there are the several volumes of *CMM* and *PMFC*, to which may be added the editions by J. Wolf (*Der Squarcialupi-Codex*, Lippstadt, 1955), T. W. Marrocco (*Fourteenth-Century Italian Cacce*, Cambridge, Mass., 2nd edn., 1961) and L. Ellinwood (*The Works of Francesco Landini*, Cambridge, Mass., 1939). See also *The Oxford Anthology: Medieval Music*, ed. N. Sandon and W. T. Marrocco (London, 1977).

Table I. *Time-values 1200–1300*[1]

A
1200–1275[2]

$\times \frac{1}{16}:$

$^{6}_{8}(^{3}_{8},\ ^{9}_{8},\ ^{12}_{8})$

B
1275–1300[3]

Franconian:

$\times \frac{1}{16}$ $\times \frac{1}{8}:$

$\frac{3}{8}$ $\frac{3}{4}$

$\times \frac{1}{8}:$

Petronian: as above, plus: Values as above, $\frac{3}{4}$ time only, plus:

(for Ars Nova interpretations, sometimes preferred by scholars, see Table II)

[1] The problems of ligatures, the *plica*, and the shorter note-values are not fully entered upon in this table, nor is the possibility of duple metre discussed.

[2] To *c.* 1300 for English music, and certain Continental idioms. For the early part of the period, the notation is non-mensural, even though specific time-values are implied.

[3] To *c.* 1350 in England.

conventional sign or a numerical ratio) are to be performed faster or slower, in the ratio indicated, than those representing a 'whole value' (*integer valor*). To take a simple example, a breve under the sign $\frac{2}{1}$ (or ¢) has the value of a semibreve in *integer valor*. This is a form of diminution, the value of the breve having been diminished to that of a semibreve. But augmentation is

Table II. *Time-values 1300–1400: France*

A
1300–1320

$\times \frac{1}{8}$

$\frac{2}{2}\left(\frac{3}{2}\right)$

$\frac{6}{4}\left(\frac{9}{4}\right)$

$\frac{2}{4}\left(\frac{3}{4}\right)$ *or*

B
1320–1400[5]

$\times \frac{1}{8}$ $\times \frac{1}{4}$ [6]

$\frac{2}{2}\left(\frac{3}{2}\right)$

$\frac{6}{4}\left(\frac{9}{4}\right)$ $\frac{2}{2}\left(\frac{3}{2}\right)$

$\frac{2}{2}\ \frac{3}{2}\ \left(\frac{6}{4},\frac{9}{4}\right)$ $\frac{2}{2}\left(\frac{3}{2}\right)$

$\frac{2}{4},\frac{3}{4}\left(\frac{6}{8},\frac{9}{8}\right)$ $\frac{2}{4}\left(\frac{6}{8},\frac{3}{4},\frac{9}{8}\right)$

$\frac{2}{4}\left(\frac{3}{4}\right)$ $\frac{6}{8}\left(\frac{9}{8}\right)$ $\frac{2}{4}\left(\frac{6}{8}\right)$ $\frac{3}{4}\left(\frac{9}{8}\right)$

$\frac{2}{4}\left(\frac{3}{4}\right)$ $\frac{2}{4}$

$\frac{6}{8}$

$\frac{6}{8}\left(\frac{9}{8}\right)$ $\frac{3}{4}$

$\frac{9}{8}$

---

[1] Range of time-values in lower parts.

[2] The *máxima* is rarely if ever perfected, but it may be used in triple mensuration and imperfected by a following *longa*, note or rest.

[3] Range of time-values in upper parts.

[4] *Prolatio maior imperfecta*: other prolations are in theory possible (see last four lines of B) but are rare in this period.

[5] After *c.* 1350 in England (cf. Table I). The minim is of constant value, so that in the last four lines its transcriptional equivalents should also be regarded as equal.

[6] This is suitable for most works of the period. For some examples of proportion and coloration, expressed in terms of black-void ('white') notation, see Table IV.

equally possible, and ratios are used which are not simple multiples: $\frac{3}{2}$ and $\frac{4}{3}$ are common. Granted that the intended ratio is unambiguous (though it often is not), the modern transcriber has two weapons at his disposal: the use of an appropriately changed scale of reduction, and the indication of a presumed tempo relationship. When proportions are used simultaneously with *integer valor*, or with each other, the relationships are obviously unambiguous: simple multiples may be reduced to the values chosen to represent *integer valor*, while more complex ratios may be shown by the most readily assimilable form of the intended cross-rhythm (in $\frac{3}{1}$, for example, by additionally halving the triple-time values, resulting in a $\frac{3}{2}$ ratio which is expressed in modern notation by ordinary triplets or by a combination of time-signatures such as $\frac{3}{4}$ and $\frac{2}{4}$).

It is when proportional writing is used successively, and not simultaneously, that a modern editor's difficulties really begin. There is the problem of interpretation — for example, the sign 3 is often found by itself and may mean either $\frac{3}{1}$ or $\frac{3}{2}$ —, and the question as to whether the composer intended a strict ratio at all. Specific answers to these questions cannot be given here: some are given in the standard books on notation, but in many cases the composer's intentions remain unclear. Up to about 1450, a strictly numerical interpretation is usually valid, and modern values may be increased or reduced accordingly. The opening of Dufay's motet 'Ecclesie militantis' will illustrate the conventions of a somewhat archaic work of the 1430s (Ex. 1, p. 22).[4] Around the middle of the century, however, it became customary to alternate passages in O (the normal triple-time signature) with passages in ₵ (the diminished duple-time signature). In such cases it is clear that the semibreve of ₵ is faster than the semibreve of O; but it is far from clear that it should be twice as fast. On pragmatic grounds it is likely that the truth lies between the two extremes: and a short passage in Dufay's Mass *L'Homme armé* (Credo, bars 84 ff.) in which the two mensurations occur simultaneously suggests 4:3 as a permissible solution when they occur consecutively. If the editor is halving the values in O, he may either halve or quarter those in ₵; but

---

[4] Transcribed from Trent MS 87. The revised edition of *CMM*, I, i contains a similarly presented version, with which this example may usefully be compared. Some of the varieties of proportion available in the early fifteenth century, and the signs used to denote them, are given in Table IV.

Table III. *Time-values 1300–1420: Italy*[1]

A   'Archaic' pieces in the notation of Marchetus

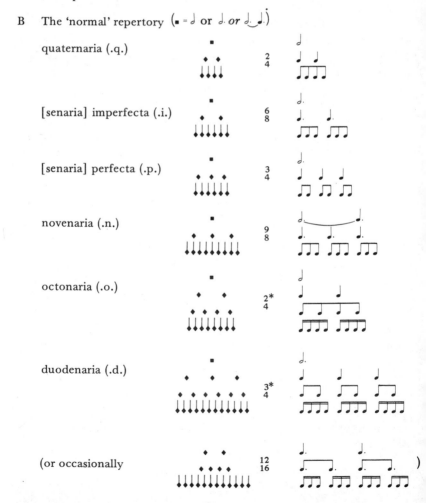

Largely confined to the Robertsbridge Codex (London, British Library, Add. 28550) and a few pieces in the Rossi Codex (Rome, Biblioteca Vaticana, Rossi 215). But the scale of reduction is also appropriate for archaic material in 'normal' notation, i.e. in which the smallest semibreves of any divisio are identified as *minimae* and consistently marked with the upward tail.

The asterisk is used to distinguish the time-signatures representing *octonaria* and *duodenaria* from those representing *quaternaria* and *senaria perfecta* respectively. On the assumption that, through French influence, the minims of the first four divisions above are theoretically of equal value, it is argued that those of *octonaria* and *duodenaria* are in the ratio 4:3 compared with those of the former; and that, consequently, $\frac{2}{4}^* = 3{:}2$ of $\frac{2}{4}$ (as indicated in the table). Some editors would use $\frac{4}{4}$ (■ = ○) and $\frac{3}{2}$ or $\frac{12}{8}$ (■ = ○.) for *octonaria* and *duodenaria* respectively.

C Re-notation of *octonaria* and *duodenaria*

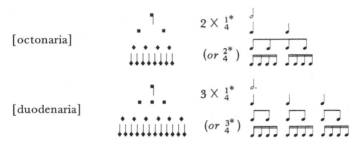

Pirrotta (*CMM*, VIII, i) regards these notations as forms of *quaternaria*, substituted for an older *octonaria* and *duodenaria*. Hoppin (*Medieval Music*, New York, 1978, p. 436) regards them as a 'more precise notation' of *octonaria* and *duodenaria*. The reader is recommended to study the introductions to the various volumes of *CMM*, VIII (*The Music of Fourteenth Century Italy*) for further information.

[1] No attempt is made to embrace the full theoretical system of Marchetus or later writers in this table. The use of the *semibrevis maior* is not here shown, while smaller values vary in the sources and cannot readily be codified. Late Italian sources borrow from French notation such devices as mensuration signs, proportions, coloration (black-void, red, red-void), and the *punctus additionis*, instead of or in combination with traditional Italian methods.

[2] 'Senaria gallica' implies French conventions for fewer than six unmarked semibreves (see Table I). Marchetus did not allow for an Italian form of *senaria imperfecta*: the only type of Italian *senaria* which he can conceive is *perfecta*. In Rossi no. 24 (*CMM*, VIII, ii, no. 29), this is marked '.sy.' for 'senaria ytalica', its minims being equivalent to the *semibreves minimae* of *senaria gallica*.

Table IV. *Time-values 1400–1450*

Proportional equivalences 1400–1450

Proportional equivalences c. 1450[6]

	$\times \dfrac{1}{4}$	$\times \dfrac{1}{2}$
¢ ◇ ≙ $\frac{3}{4}$ of O ◇	$\frac{2}{4}$ ♩ ≙ $\frac{3}{4}$ of $\frac{3}{4}$ ♩	$\frac{2}{2}$ ♩ ≙ $\frac{3}{4}$ of $\frac{3}{2}$ ♩
	or $\frac{2}{4}$ ♩ ≐ $\frac{3}{4}$ of $\frac{3}{2}$ ♩	
O2 □ ≙ $\frac{3}{2}$ of O ◇	$\frac{3}{2}$ ♩ ≙ $\frac{3}{2}$ of $\frac{3}{4}$ ♩	$\frac{3}{1}$ ○ ≙ $\frac{3}{2}$ of $\frac{3}{2}$ ♩
	or $\frac{3}{2}$ ♩ ≐ $\frac{3}{2}$ of $\frac{3}{2}$ ♩	
3, $\frac{3}{2}$ etc. ◇ = $\frac{2}{3}$ of ¢ (*or* C) ◇	$\frac{3}{4}$ ♩ = $\frac{2}{3}$ of $\frac{2}{4}$ ♩	$\frac{3}{2}$ ♩ = $\frac{2}{3}$ of $\frac{2}{2}$ ♩
	or $\frac{3}{4}$ ♩ ≐ $\frac{2}{3}$ of $\frac{2}{2}$ ♩	
3, $\frac{3}{1}$ etc. ◇ = $\frac{1}{3}$ of ¢ (*or* C) ◇	$\frac{3}{4}$ ♩ = $\frac{1}{3}$ of $\frac{2}{4}$ ♩	$\frac{3}{2}$ ♩ = $\frac{1}{3}$ of $\frac{2}{2}$ ♩
	or $\frac{3}{4}$ ♩ ≐ $\frac{1}{3}$ of $\frac{2}{2}$ ♩	

Other proportions as indicated numerically or as evident from simultaneous occurrence.[7]

---

[1] Range of time-values in lower parts (tenor and contratenor).

[2] In this column, for $\frac{2}{4}$ bar-lengths can throughout be doubled and $\frac{4}{4}$ used.

[3] Range of values in upper parts; minim equivalence applies.

[4] See Anon. XII in *CS*, iii, 483. From this point onwards the reductions in column 2 apply to the visual values of the original notation, not to a hypothetical *integer valor*. Cf. note 5.

[5] See Anon. XI in *CS*, iii, 473. Practical instances occur in C. Van den Borren, *Polyphonia Sacra* (rev. edn., London, 1962), 53–74 (Gloria and Credo by Binchois). The editor uses halved values in O and C, quartered values in Φ and Ɔ and eighthed values in ♭, so a possible metronomic rate would be as follows: ♩ = 60 in O and C; ♩ = 90 in Φ, ♩ = 80 in Ɔ, ♪ = 100 in ♭.

[6] For the first of these ratios, see above, p. 17. The alternative forms of modern transcription (i.e. quartered values for the faster-moving originals, halved for the slower) are the more common in each case.

[7] A great range of possibilities is given in the theoretical works of Tinctoris and Gafurius. The distinction between 3:2 (*sesquialtera*) and 3:1 (*tripla*) is often unclear in sources, a wide variety of signs being employed.

Ex. 1. Dufay, 'Ecclesie militantis', extracts

he ought in either case to suggest an appropriate tempo ratio (see Chapter 1). A typical situation, and its possible solution, may be illustrated by the Kyrie of Busnois' Mass *O crux lignum*, a work possibly of the 1460s or even later (Ex. 2, p. 24).[5]

Signs of mensuration and proportion are rarely found in sources written before 1400. When they occur at the beginning of a piece or a movement, they may be part of the material shown on preliminary staves, if these are to be used.[6] Otherwise, and for subsequent changes, they should be shown above the staff to which they refer (see above, p. 11). It is not good practice to give them in place of modern signatures, since their meaning is different. The preliminary staves may also show the first note, or the initial phrase, in the original notation; but this is not a substitute for indicating the scale of reduction, since such devices as ligatures, proportion, or coloration may disguise their significance. The scale of reduction may be discussed in the editorial commentary, or it may be indicated above the score in some such form as $\downarrow$ = $\blacksquare$. Such devices as $\times\frac{1}{8}$, $\times\frac{1}{4}$ (or for that matter $\div 8$, $\div 4$), while unambiguous in the majority of cases, become confusing when proportions enter into the question, and are therefore better avoided (their use in Tables I–V illustrates how readily they could be misunderstood in isolation).[7] The reduction of values in proportional passages should be shown when necessary in terms of the visual relationship, not of the real or supposed *integer valor*.

Many editors of the comparatively recent past have employed original note-values (for *integer valor* and for quasi-*integer valor* signs such as ₵ when used independently) in fifteenth-century music. For music written earlier in the century, this practice suffers from the general disadvantages already mentioned. Even with a composer such as Ockeghem, the use of simple and double augmentation in certain passages has led his distinguished and scrupulous editor into the doubling and quadrupling of the composer's own written note-values in those places.[8] Towards

---

[5] From *Cw*, cxxiii, ed. D. W. Shipley (Wolfenbüttel, n.d.); tempo indications and ratios added by the present writer. Apart from this omission (throughout the Mass), the edition has been made with exemplary care and illustrates the use of *Mensurstrich* (below, p. 49) at its most sophisticated.

[6] See above, p. 10.

[7] They are also unsuitable in transcribing from modal notation (see below, pp. 37–8), for which an explanation in the commentary is essential.

[8] *Collected Works*, ed. D. Plamenac; e.g. vol. i (2nd edn., American Musicological Society, 1959), pp. 114–16, from the Mass *L'Homme armé*.

Ex. 2. Busnois, Mass *O crux lignum*, extract from *Kyrie*

the end of the century, nevertheless, this particular problem recedes into the background, and the use of original note-values everywhere (except in passages employing simultaneous diminution or augmentation), as for example in the editions of Obrecht and Josquin by Wolf and Smijers respectively, carries conviction. Though the most recent practice favours the halving of values for music of this period, the older method permits a closer involvement with the composers themselves and their way of work.

The reduction of time-values increases the extent to which the editor must take responsibility for translating the separate notes of his sources into cross-beamed groups. In many cases the solution will be obvious enough, or will be settled by the demands of syllabification (see below, p. 42), unless of course the editor adopts beaming across syllable changes. But there will remain many instances in which he will have to decide how much interpretation to offer through patterns of beaming suggestive of accentuation and articulation. Only general advice (applicable also to Renaissance music) can be offered here. It is important to guard against over-interpretation. If there is any doubt, it is best to stick to standard patternings, limiting the cross-beam to simple subdivisions of the bar (e.g. ♫♫♫ ♫♫♫ rather than ♫♫ ♫♫♫). Only the clearest cases of syncopation or cross-rhythm (such as hemiola patterns in $\frac{6}{8}$ time) should be

Table V. *Time-values 1450–1600*

A
1450–1500

Primary values as in Table IV. But ⊙ and ₵ acquire the meaning of augmentation, while ₵ and, eventually, Ⓓ become 'normal' signs (thus giving ⊙ and ₵ the character of double augmentation, i.e. an apparent increase in value by four). The following equivalences can be inferred:

	$\times \frac{1}{4}$	$\times \frac{1}{2}$
Ⓓ ◇ ≙ $\frac{3}{2}$ ₵ (C) ◇	$\frac{3}{4}$ ♩ ≙ $\frac{3}{2}$ of $\frac{4}{4}$ ♩	$\frac{3}{2}$ ♩ ≙ $\frac{3}{2}$ of $\frac{2}{2}$ ♩
	or $\frac{4}{4}$ ♩ ≙ $\frac{2}{3}$ of $\frac{3}{2}$ ♩	
₵ □ = C (O) ◇ = ₵ (O) ♩	$\frac{2}{4}$ ♩	$\frac{2}{2}$ ○
Occasionally: Ⓓ ◇ = ₵ ◇	$\frac{3}{4}$ ♩ = $\frac{2}{4}$ ♩	$\frac{3}{2}$ ♩ = $\frac{2}{2}$ ♩
Ⓓ □ = O ◇	$\frac{3}{4}$ ♩	$\frac{3}{2}$ ♩

B
1500–1600

	$\times \frac{1}{2}$	$\times 1$
₵ □ ◇ ♩	$\frac{2}{2}$ ○ ♩ ♩	₵ ▭ ○ ♩
C □ ≙ ₵ □ ¹	$\frac{2}{2}$ ○	C ($\frac{4}{2}$) ▭
C ♩ ≙ ₵ ♩ ²		$\frac{4}{4}$ (C) ♩

For *sesquialtera* and *tripla* see Table IV and note 7 there. For some peculiarities of English notation of this period, see the introductory remarks in the appropriate volumes of *MB* and *EECM*.

[1] This refers primarily to the preference of late sixteenth-century English composers for C in view of the substantial slowing-down of tempo by then.
[2] This refers to Italian madrigals 'a note nere', for which a transcription in unreduced values is appropriate.

indicated by the beaming.[9] The use of *Mensurstrich* (below, p. 49) does naturally inhibit the use of the tie, but, even there, care should be taken to avoid the appearance of factitious complexity.

The discussion of time-values leads naturally to the consideration of barring and the means of indicating it. Very little music before 1500 has bar-lines (fifteenth-century keyboard music is an exception), though the spacing of groups of notes, the use of the *punctus divisionis*, and the application of fifteenth-century *tactus* theory provide partial equivalents. In general, however, the modern editor has a free hand in such matters. For music of the early thirteenth century, compound duple time ($\frac{6}{8}$ for preference) most nearly corresponds to the musical realities, though the occasional bar of $\frac{9}{8}$ will often be required, while a $\frac{12}{8}$ barring is suited to a number of works. The editor must be guided by his feeling for the underlying pulse: the notation of the period offers no clues. A recent editor of Perotinus, Ethel Thurston, has used bar-lines only to mark off the ends of sections. While the result is not inelegant in appearance, the method makes reference difficult, confuses the notation of accidentals, and leaves the performer without guidance as to underlying rhythmic pulse.

In the later thirteenth century, when the scale of reduction is changed to one-eighth of the original, $\frac{3}{4}$ time is usually best. Tischler in his recent edition of the late thirteenth-century repertory of the Montpellier MS (3 vols.; Madison: A–R Editions, 1978) has used longer bars, basing his choice on the phrasing of the upper parts. This seems to me a mistake. The underlying rhythmic structure of a motet is controlled by its tenor, and the use of longer bars ($\frac{6}{4}$ or $\frac{9}{4}$) could be logically governed only by its patterns.

As the period progresses, bar-lengths will gradually decrease in accordance with the reduced values of the original notation; in real terms, and in accordance with the editorial range of note-values, they will remain fairly constant. But it is impossible to lay down strict rules. Original signs of mensuration and

---

[9] For the special problems of late fourteenth-century music see Apel, *The Notation of Polyphonic Music* (5th edn., Cambridge, Mass., 1953), pp. 395–435, and his *French Secular Music of the Late Fourteenth Century* (Cambridge, Mass., 1950). Slightly simpler methods are adopted in his later edition, *French Secular Compositions of the Fourteenth Century* (CMM, LIII).

proportion, the *punctus divisionis*, and *tactus* theory do not in themselves provide a solution to the question of barring: followed strictly, they often produce inconveniently short bars. But editorial barring should not normally conflict with them. There is no place for the whimsical following of the phrasing of a single part. Barring should express the underlying pulse of the music in its totality. Yet there may be exceptions even to this general principle. The upper parts of fourteenth-century motets may legitimately be barred more frequently than their slow-moving tenors and contratenors. In a work like Ockeghem's *Missa prolationum*, on the other hand, the mensurations of the individual voice-parts may be thought to conceal a basic pulse which in an edition in score ought to take precedence over their metrical peculiarities.

The usefulness of barring is in proportion to its legibility and its regularity. Historically, barring arose in the medieval period and took the form of a vertical straight line through the whole score.[10] There is little reason to adopt any other method in music up to 1450. The advantages and disadvantages of *Mensurstrich* will be discussed in the following chapter. It is possible and often desirable for an editor and his publisher to exhibit larger aspects of musical structure (which can be an extension of metre) through the layout on the page—as has been done very successfully, for instance, in the *Musica Britannica* edition of the works of Dunstable.[11]

The questions of clefs, transposition, and accidentals must now be considered. Until quite recently, many editors used a variety of C, F, and G clefs in apparent accord with the usage of their sources. But this accord, because of the variable number of lines on the medieval staff, was sometimes more apparent than real; and a literal observance, even when possible, sometimes necessitated frequent changes of clef. The more extreme effects of such a policy can be seen in Plamenac's edition of Ockeghem. I can see little need, for music up to 1450, for the use of any clefs other than treble, bass, and 'transposed treble' (𝄞). This is true even for instrumental music, which has to be presented in a

---

10 See, e.g., Faenza, Biblioteca comunale, MS 117 (*c.* 1400); modern edition by D. Plamenac, *CMM*, LVII.

11 *MB*, viii, ed. M. F. Bukofzer (2nd rev. edn. prepared by M. Bent, I. Bent and B. Trowell, 1970).

form suited to many different kinds of instrument. There is little point in considering the special claims of (say) the player of a large medieval fiddle or of the modern viola if the music is just as likely to be transposed and played on a recorder. Nor can I see the justification for rigorously excluding the transposed treble clef as well as C clefs. An all-purpose clef of medium range is a necessity for most medieval music, and this particular one will readily serve the purposes of music originally written in the alto (c'^3) or tenor c'^4) clefs.[12]

There is little point in making transposed editions of medieval music. Though there is no justification for regarding its written pitch as being linked in any way to our standard of $a' = 440$ c.p.s. —indeed pitch should be thought of as purely relative except in the case of organ music—, transposition compromises one of its great strengths, which is its adaptability for different forces. For the same reason any other form of editorial tampering with a view to particular circumstances of performance is to be deprecated. If transposition is considered essential, it is better to stick to the primary intervals—the 4th and the 5th—, though medieval scribes did themselves on occasion use the written transposition of a tone.[13]

The question of accidentals is not so easily answered. The whole subject has two sides to it: what the sources actually say, and what is justifiable by way of editorial supplementation (or suppression). It is essential to gain a clear idea of the first. The medieval treatment of accidentals was quite different from ours. In the first place, there was no clear distinction between accidentals and key-signatures, though there was a tendency towards making one which resulted ultimately in our present-day conventions. Secondly, a medieval accidental, even if in the apparent position of a key-signature, applied only to the pitch-level at which it appeared; moreover, a 'key-signature' might well appear in one part but not in others. Thirdly, an accidental

[12] Voices may be identified numerically or named according to historically appropriate conventions. Some examples, with recommended abbreviations, are given in Appendix II. Score layout will normally be in order of pitch; if a tenor and contra-tenor share the same range, the tenor should appear below.

[13] The earliest such example (as opposed to the transposition of a mode or a cantus firmus) appears to be the keyboard version of the motet 'Tribum que non abhorruit' from the *Roman de Fauvel* (Paris, Bibl. nat., MS f. fr. 146; ed. L. Schrade, *PMFC*, i, p. 54) in the Robertsbridge fragment of *c.* 1375 (London, Brit. Lib., Add. MS 28550; ed. W. Apel, *CEKM*, i, no. 5), in which the original is transposed up one tone.

might appear at some distance before the note which it was intended to inflect: since it might also be displaced on the staff, or might appear directly above or below the note affected, there is ample scope for misunderstanding. Finally, a flat might be cancelled by a sharp sign, and a sharp by a flat; and the early form of the sharp sign looks like a natural (the two are, historically, identical).

The diligent transcriber will faithfully record the vagaries of his source, but in an edition for publication some compromise is inevitable. Let us first consider key-signatures. A useful rule of thumb is to interpret an accidental or combination of accidentals, standing at the beginning of a staff, either in conjunction with a clef or (as the *b ♭* sometimes is) on its own, as a key-signature. By a natural extension, an accidental given with a clef-change within a line may be regarded as a 'signature'. (Clearly a *b ♭* standing alone within a line can also admit of this interpretation.) If this 'signature' is consistently stated throughout a piece it may be translated into a modern key-signature; if however it occurs only intermittently, it may be better to treat it as an accidental with 'prolonged validity' (see below).

The relatively limited 'vertical' scope of a medieval accidental is also a matter of difficulty. Musicians nowadays can accept the convention of 'partial signatures' (except perhaps in keyboard music), whereby one part may have a different key-signature from another. Indeed, it can serve much the same pragmatic purpose as was originally intended. But it is harder in a modern score to convey the sense that a signature refers only to the specific octave-pitches at which it occurs, and the present-day consensus is that it is not worth the attempt to do so. The printing of an accidental in a key-signature at a pitch at variance with that of modern convention will no doubt give the impression that that specific pitch only is intended; but if its position on the staff happens to coincide with that of modern convention, octave-duplication will be implied. For better or worse, therefore, a modern key-signature, within the context of the individual staff, should be printed in the modern way and be considered to carry its modern meaning. Cancellations arising from this must be indicated in small print.

Medieval source accidentals which are not capable of interpretation as a 'key-signature' may nevertheless have a force beyond that of modern convention. Since most medieval sources are unbarred, the distinction cannot be quantified; but the point is that there is no reason to equate their force with that of the modern bar-line. The extent of the validity of an accidental in a medieval source is a question which an editor must decide for himself on the basis of his knowledge and experience, independently of the exigencies of transcription. How to deal with the resulting discrepancies will be considered below. When the editor is certain as to what his sources say, he can then decide to what extent they need to be supplemented. The complexities of this subject far exceed the scope of this book. One or two general points may be made, however. Medieval theorists' discussions of *musica ficta* (or *musica falsa*) are only partly relevant to the matter in hand. Arising in the first place, in treatises of the thirteenth century, out of discussions of the semitone, they exclude the b♭ (or b'♭) from consideration, since this was considered to be part of the diatonic system (*musica recta* or *musica vera*).[14] Nor on the whole, whatever they may say about the necessity of *musica ficta*, do the treatises concern themselves specifically with what ought to be added by a performer in relation to the readings of a written source. Their speculations for the most part have an abstract air about them. It is possible to argue, for large tracts of the medieval repertory, that there is no general conspiracy to omit necessary accidentals. Inconsistencies can often be explained on the basis of changes of lineation in copying (an obvious fruitful source of error), or on the basis of simple inaccuracy. It is a healthy modern tendency to restrict editorial additions to the barest necessities, though it can be a matter of opinion as to what these are.[15]

[14] On the significance of medieval accidentals for solmization, see M. Bent, 'Musica Ficta and Musica Recta', *MD*, xxxvi (1972), pp. 73–100.

[15] The most important theoretical sources include the following: Johannes de Garlandia, *Introductio musicae* (*CS*, i, 157–75), p. 166; Magister Lambertus (*CS*, i, 251–81), p. 258; Anon. II, ibid., p. 310; Philippe de Vitry, Marchetus de Padua, Nicholas of Capua, Johannes de Muris, and Prosdocimus de Beldemandis. From the later fifteenth century onwards one may cite Tinctoris (a few references in the *Liber de arte contrapuncti* and a problematic definition in the *Diffinitorium*), Ugolino of Orvieto (*Declaratio musicae disciplinae*, II, xxxiv, and *Tractatus monochordi*, viii–x), Gafori (*Practica musicae*, Milan, 1496, III, xiii), Pietro Aaron (*Il Toscanello in musica*, Venice, 1523, discussed by Reese, *Music in the Renaissance*, p. 182), S. Vanneo (*Recanetum in musica aurea*, Rome, 1533, esp. III, xiv, xxxvi, xxxvii), G. M. Lanfranco (*Scintille di musica*, Brescia, 1533), G. Zarlino (esp. *L'istituzioni harmoniche*, Venice, 1573), and the Spanish theorists F. Tovar (*Libro de musica practica*, Barcelona, 1510), J. Bermudo (*Declaración*, Osuna, 1555) and T. de Santa María (*Arte de tañer fantasia*,Valladolid, 1556). Most of these are available in

The preceding comments reveal the need for a system which will preserve the readings of the source while remaining true to the principles of a transcription into 'modern notation'. The configuration of clefs and key-signatures at the start of a piece can most conveniently be shown on preliminary staves; subsequent changes should be noted in the commentary. The key-signatures, if any, are then translated into their nearest modern equivalent so far as the individual staff is concerned, while permitting variation from one staff to another ('partial signatures'). How often, if at all, may one change the 'modern' signature? The answer must be decided by the editor on pragmatic grounds. In one modern edition of an exceptionally high standard (*The Eton Choirbook*, edited by F. Ll. Harrison, *MB*, x–xii), all manuscript changes are preserved, but are moved to the beginning or end of the modern printed line in which they occur (the precise points of change being noted in the commentary). It might be argued, however, that the result can be confusing, and the system for accidentals about to be described eliminates the need for frequent change.

Four kinds of accidental are needed. Those in large type are in the source, or are admitted from another source of suitable authority (if this is consonant with the kind of overall editorial policy being adopted—accidentals from another source *could* be regarded as editorial; the commentary should note divergences which cannot be incorporated in the score).[16] Small accidentals are those which are implied but not stated in the source. This might arise from the difference between the medieval and modern conventions as to key-signatures; or from an editorial view as to the extent of the validity of an accidental expressed in the source, either by extending it beyond the (editorial) bar in which it occurs or by cancelling it within the bar. The context

---

the editions *CS, GS, CSM,* or in facsimile reprints. Modern discussions include those of H. Tischler, ' "Musica Ficta" in the Thirteenth Century', *ML*, liv (1973), pp. 38–56; R. Bray, 'The Interpretation of Musica Ficta in English Music *c*. 1490–*c*. 1580', *PRMA*, xcviii (1971–2), pp. 113–22; S. Rubio, *Classical Polyphony* (Oxford, 1972, on the Spanish theorists); M. Bent, op. cit.; M. Bent and A. Hughes in their edition of the 'Old Hall' Manuscript (*CMM*, XLVI); and F. Ll. Harrison in his edition of the Eton Choirbook (*MB*, x–xii, introduction in vol. x). Bent, Hughes, and Bray have favoured a liberal, Harrison and Doe a sparing application of editorial accidentals, at least in English music.

[16] Sharps or flats should however be replaced in appropriate cases by the natural sign, as should clefs occasionally used for that purpose (e.g. in English sixteenth-century keyboard music).

will always reveal which use is intended.[17] Purely editorial accidentals should be printed (small) above or below the staff. All these should be used in accordance with the modern convention of validity within the bar. Finally, by a useful recent innovation, round brackets may be used to enclose cautionary accidentals, i.e. ones which are not strictly required by modern convention but which the performer might overlook.

This apparently complex system nevertheless works well in practice. Its object, of course, is to place all the facts in front of the performer or reader, so that where an editorial opinion is involved the performer is at liberty to substitute his own. Two further kinds of information are needed, however. First, it is necessary to indicate the beginning of each new line in each part in the sole or primary source, so that the performer can assess for himself the editor's interpretation of the extent to which accidentals remain valid. This may be done in the commentary, which in any case will need to note changes of 'key-signature' in the sense just defined, but it can if desired be accommodated quite unobtrusively in the score itself by a symbol such as NL above the staff at the appropriate point. Second, it is important to indicate the presence in the source of accidentals which are redundant according to the modern conventions of the editorial barred score. These too may be given in the commentary, but in music of the period under consideration (except for keyboard) they are likely to be few and far between, and the present writer's inclination is to incorporate them into the printed score. The incidence of 'redundant' accidentals is normally greater in Renaissance and Baroque music, and the question is more fully dealt with in the next two chapters (pages 59, 76–80), where various possible solutions are proposed (see also Appendix IV).

It will no doubt be of some comfort to the reader who has travelled thus far to be assured that this is as sophisticated a system as any music will require. On the whole, the advice given in subsequent chapters will represent a simplification, as notation progressively becomes closer to present-day methods.

Now that the major questions of editorial policy have been dealt with, the remainder of this chapter will be devoted to the

---

[17] Some editors have nevertheless distinguished accidentals consequent upon the differences between medieval (or Renaissance) and modern usage as to key-signatures by writing a full-sized accidental with a dot above.

special needs of particular repertories, and to certain remaining points of presentation.

The editing of plainsong from early manuscripts in neumes is a subject beyond the scope of this book. There is little agreement about aims and methods, even in quarters where the need for such editing is admitted. This also applies to early tropes and sequences, and to polyphonic repertories such as that of the Winchester Troper,[18] where the process of editing borders on that of imaginative guesswork. But there is something to be said for considering the special problems of monophony at a later period, and the introduction of a legible staff notation during the course of the twelfth century makes that a suitable starting-point. Moreover, the principles established for monophony will be equally applicable to non-mensurable polyphony.

By far the greater bulk of medieval monody is written in a notation which is non-mensural in the sense that its shapes and forms do not indicate specific rhythms. The question as to whether the music itself is in a free or a strict rhythm (ascertainable by other criteria) is another matter, and one for the judgement of the editor. (An intermediate form of rhythmic notation, based on ligature groupings, was devised for use in polyphonic music before the establishment of a truly mensural system in the late thirteenth century; it is conveniently labelled 'modal notation' and its correct interpretation is a matter which calls for considerable expertise on the editor's part.)

If the editor opts for a free rhythmic interpretation of monody written in non-mensural notation (as he is likely to do for liturgical plainsong and certain other categories), the best modern notation for most purposes is a series of tail-less black noteheads. An alternative is to use quavers, beamed or unbeamed according to such criteria as syllabification, accent, or ligature groupings in the source. Syllabification, however, does not require specific notational help (though I shall argue against the notational hindrance of beaming across syllable changes); accent is preferably indicated, if at all, in the verbal text; and ligature groupings are better shown by methods which can be retained in mensurable music. A final possibility for liturgical music is

18 Cambridge, Corpus Christi College, MS 473. See A. Holschneider, *Die organa von Winchester* (Hildesheim, 1968).

simply to retain traditional plainchant notation on the four-line staff.

In fact, tail-less black notes are widely accepted. In non-mensural notation of this period, there is no significance in the distinction between tailed and untailed notes, nor in the various shapes of ligature. Ligatures, however, must certainly be shown as such. It has been customary to do this, in liturgical plainsong and in comparable types of music, by means of curved slurs. These have often been confused with editorial slurs to mark syllable changes (with which they frequently coincide); and they do not distinguish between ligatures proper, in which the constituent notes are physically joined together, and forms such as the *climacus* and its descendant the *conjunctura*, in which the notes as it were 'belong' together but are not physically joined (e.g. ❜••). The former confusion can be eliminated by dispensing with 'syllable' slurs altogether. The latter distinction can very easily be preserved by using ⌐⎺⎺⌐ for true ligatures and either the curved slur or ⌐----⌐ for the others. Such a form as ❜•, can be shown by ⸍•• or ⸍•• . These methods have the advantage of being available for polyphony written in modal (or certain early forms of mensural) notation, where the distinction can be of significance.

Of all the various nuances available in staffless neumes, only one, the liquescent, or *plica* (as it came to be known), was retained in staff notation.[19] This innocent-looking sign has given musicologists a lot of trouble. Plainsong scholars, relying solely on the phonological contexts in which it occurs, have suggested two radically opposed methods of performance,[20] while those interested in polyphony have had to make do with a puzzling remark by Magister Lambertus, to the effect that it is performed by the epiglottis.[21] It may appear either as a single note (e.g. ⎩, ❜, or ⎤) or as a double note (e.g. ⎘⎩). There seems to be no difference between them, and the form ⸝⸜ will cover all. But the editor has to decide at what pitch the subsidiary note should be performed: the manuscript forms indicate either a downwards or an upwards direction; but they do not indicate the precise

---

[19] The *quilisma* is retained in the Solesmes editions of plainchant, but it is not found in medieval sources in staff-notation.

[20] See the discussion in W. Apel, *Gregorian Chant* (London, n.d.), pp. 104–6.

[21] 'Fit autem plica in voce per compositionem epiglotti cum repercussione gutturis subtiliter inclusa' (*CS*, i, 273). As to pitch, Lambertus and others say only that the subsidiary note 'divides' the interval between the main note and the one following.

interval, and simple prolongation of the main note is an occasional possibility. The context, and the editor's expertise, will have to decide the matter.

Music without bar-lines slightly complicates the procedure previously outlined for the treatment of accidentals, though in practice the solution will normally be found to be straightforward. All accidentals (except those in a key-signature) should be taken, in the edition, as belonging only to the note which they precede. All those given in the source are printed in full size (unless the editor disagrees with them, in which case they are transferred to the commentary). The editor then uses either small accidentals before the note, or accidentals above the staff, according to his judgement as to the extent to which they reflect the reading of the source, for any supplementation. Cautionary accidentals, if needed, should be in round brackets.

The method of transcription just outlined is suitable for non-mensurable polyphony, such as that of the St Martial school, as well as for monophonic music. But an editor may well wish to suggest specific rhythms in editing monophonic music, and there are, broadly speaking, two ways of doing this. They can be indicated above the non-mensural black notes by means of pitchless symbols: this has the advantage of not committing too deeply the performer who may have different ideas. Alternatively —and this is much the commoner method—the rhythms may be incorporated into the transcription itself. This need create no ambiguity; ligatures should be indicated in one of the ways already outlined. Such a procedure implies a greater conviction on the part of the editor and makes it harder for the performer to resist his interpretation.

Some repertories of monophonic music are, indeed, written in a form of mensural notation—the *Cantigas de Santa María*, the songs of the *Chansonnier Cangé*, and so on—and in that case the transcription follows the methods adopted for mensural polyphony. But the mensural notation of these sources is often ambiguous in various respects, and a fuller than usual editorial note will normally be required to explain the degree of choice made by the editor in the solution of rhythmic problems. Where a metrical rendering has been given of music in a non-mensural notation, that fact should of course be stated.

The polyphony of the Notre Dame school (Leoninus, Perotinus, and their contemporaries and successors) presents its own special problems. In two-part *organum*, in which the upper part moves swiftly against a sustained tenor, there is some disagreement among scholars as to whether the parts are to be sung metrically or not. They may be presented either non-mensurally or with specific rhythms. In the latter case the solution will depend partly on the grouping of ligatures (the notation being regarded as fundamentally 'modal'), and it is particularly important that these should be noted. The methods already given enable the transcriber to distinguish clearly between the descending three-note ligature and its close cousin the *conjunctura*, derived from the plainsong *climacus*. The method of indicating rhythms above the staff is less suitable here, partly because in polyphony it clutters the score, and partly because in this type of music the sustained-note polyphony usually alternates with sections in which the rhythms are specified. Indeed, most *conductus* and many early motets rely on conjecture for the establishment of rhythm: but the conjecture rests on a solid basis of scholarship and in the certainty that a fixed metre was intended. In such cases it would be ridiculous to present the music in any but clearly defined rhythms, though alternative interpretations are sometimes possible and may be indicated above the staff.

Notre Dame sustained-note *organum* provides our earliest examples of a style in which (editorial) barring is not applicable to all the parts. The sustained notes in the tenor are best presented as breves or semibreves, separated by a bar-line whenever the change of note corresponds to one in the upper part or parts (for these considerations apply equally to the fixed-rhythm, sustained-note sections of three- and four-part *organum*). The chopping up of the sustained notes into shorter ones, connected by ties, is much less clear to the eye.

The Notre Dame sources also make use of the so-called *Silbenstrich*, a short vertical stroke used to improve co-ordination and as the equivalent of rests, as well as to mark off syllable changes. Its equivalent in transcriptions is, according to the context, either a rest (of any appropriate length) or a sign of separation such as the comma; alternatively, and perhaps preferably, a short vertical stroke comparable to that in the sources may be used.

The transcriptions of *organum duplum* given in William Waite's book *The Rhythm of Twelfth-Century Polyphony* illustrate most of the points mentioned, and come near to editorial perfection. The *Oxford Anthology: Medieval Music* offers acceptable methods over a wider range of Notre Dame forms, as indeed it does for medieval music generally.

With the advent of a clear and comprehensive system of rhythmic notation in the later thirteenth century, the editing of medieval music becomes amenable to the basic principles previously outlined. Various problems of interpretation remain, but they are not such as to overshadow the whole basis of the edition. A few further points of detail follow.

The scholarly basis for the barring of medieval music has already been discussed. If the style demands different bar-lengths in different parts, only the shorter bars should be numbered or, in some styles, those which predominate or effectively control the metrical flow of the music. If the structure of the music can be clarified by editorial layout, this should certainly be done: and the task of the printer will be greatly eased if the editor's layout can be reproduced on the printed page as it stands.

Medieval keyboard music is usually barred in the sources in accordance with the metre of the music. It makes sense to retain this in the edition: a superfluous or misplaced bar-line can be indicated by a short vertical stroke overhead, and a missing one can be indicated by a dotted bar-line in the score.

The notation of ligatures has been referred to above. I am strongly of the opinion that they should be indicated in all music of the medieval period. Their insertion prevents incorrect redistribution of the syllables by the performer, and it will also hinder incorrect articulation. Some editors consider them an over-encouragement to articulate, and positively misleading in music written in 'modal' notation. But it is precisely in that context that their absence conceals the evidence for the inter-pretation of a doubtful passage.

After the disappearance of the *conjunctura* around 1320 the only sign required for ligatures (except in plainsong) is the usual ⌐‾‾⌐. When the first and/or last note of a ligature is tied in the modern edition, it is not necessary for the sign to embrace the notes connected by the tie. Ligatures are best drawn above the staff, so as not to impede any text, and at an angle to it, to avoid visual confusion. They may be omitted over groups of notes already joined by a cross-beam; but this inhibits the use of the cross-beam in other contexts, and I prefer to see the ligature sign retained even here.

The *plica* continues in use in mensural music, where to the problem of deciding on its pitch is added that of deciding on its length relative to the main note. It is possible to evade the problem, as some editors do, by writing an *acciaccatura*: I prefer a small note of a value decided by the editor. The modern fashion of writing a stroke through the stem of a plicated note arose perhaps from the difficulty of distinguishing between a small note and a full-sized note in manuscripts which were, perhaps, to be reproduced photographically for publication; but its use in proper printed music seems undesirable. (A useful convention in preparing manuscripts for the printer is to write 'small' material in red, or at least to draw a red ring around it.)

Coloration (the use of red notes in the context of full-black notation, or of black ones in the context of black-void—i.e. 'white'—notation) is conventionally indicated, nowadays, by ⌐ ¬. Such signs as ⌐ ¬ and ⌐ ¬ can indicate white-void and red-void coloration (in full-black notation), and must of course be explained in the notes. Coloration ought certainly to be indicated; it can serve to indicate probable tempo relationships and accentuation to the knowledgeable, and may in any case be important evidence of a composer's musical thought. Coloration was the medieval composer's main weapon against a purely arithmetical view of time relationships. Needless to say, this does not apply to the short note-values in black-void notation: indeed there is an important distinction, which the editor has it in his power to clarify, between (say) a black minim and a crotchet in 'white' notation, identical though they usually are in appearance.[22]

Repeats can be indicated by the conventional modern signs, though it should be explained in the commentary what it is in the source to which they correspond, or indeed if they are purely editorial. Medieval repeats are mostly found in connection with first- and second-time bars, marked 'ouvert' and 'clos' (or 'aperto' and 'chiuso') in the manuscripts. These indications are often badly misplaced, however. On the whole it is best to use the modern signs, and either to include the original instructions in

---

[22] The uncoloured crotchet may of course appear as ♪ in 'white' notation, corresponding to the ♪ of black notation, from which sign its English name derived.

the score precisely where they occur in the source or, failing
that, to state in the commentary when adjustment was found
to be necessary.

In *estampies*, one often finds instructions to repeat whole
sections in a later *punctus*, itself to be repeated with first- and
second-time bars. The resulting complexities can be seen in Nos.
84 and 86 of the *Oxford Anthology: Medieval Music*, where the
notation of the sources is reproduced. On the whole it seems
best to write out such passages in full, perhaps marking them
with angle brackets as explained below.

This brings us to the question of lacunae. Unless one is
avowedly printing a fragment, an attempt must of course be
made to restore the text. Square brackets are the traditional
method, but some publishers prefer small notes. There is,
however, a distinction to be drawn between omissions by the
scribe and lacunae consequent upon damage to the source. One
could very intelligibly use square brackets for the former and
small notes for the latter—or vice versa—provided an explanation
is given. Yet another situation is that described in the previous
paragraph: the writing out in full of a scribal abbreviation. For
this, angle brackets < > are recommended (see Appendix I).

Any edition of music requiring liturgical plainsong in alter-
nation should certainly include it, properly edited from sources
close in time and liturgical milieu to the polyphony itself. It is
surprising how often this requirement is overlooked: it is true
that suitable plainsong sources are not always readily available,
but the readings of modern Roman chant are often considerably
at variance from what the circumstances require. However, it is
better to use them than to omit the chant altogether (which
would be analogous to leaving out the spoken dialogue from a
Singspiel because it is not in the musical source).

A fully annotated edition will include, as an appendix, the
plainsongs of all cantus firmus pieces, and any other *cantus prius
factus* ('pre-existent material', to use our ugly modern expression). It is also a good idea to include the tenors of motets in
their original notation, as in the *Musica Britannica* edition
of Dunstable: this serves to elucidate structure and can save
laborious explanations in the commentary.[23]

---

[23] The commentary should of course identify *cantus prius factus* and specify
liturgical function when appropriate and possible.

I have left until the end of this chapter a discussion of what usually proves to be the knottiest problem of all for the conscientious editor of medieval music: the presentation of the verbal texts. Except for familiar and frequently edited material, most musicologists will require expert advice in this field. I certainly do myself. But the very process of collaboration raises one danger: the assumption that the establishment of a critical and comprehensible verbal text is a *sine qua non*. A moment's thought will convince one that this is not so, for a composer may easily set a corrupt text, with scant regard to its meaning or versification.[24] The editor's task is to purge his text of scribal corruption, but not to correct the composer. This is not an easy, nor always even a possible, distinction to make; but an understanding collaborator can do much to smooth the path.

Provençal songs raise this problem in an acute form, for they mostly survive in northern French copies of late date: their orthography is peculiar, and the linguistic forms are often corrupt. In such a case, the 'aim of the edition' must be considered: is it to revive the songs as current at the time and place of the source, or is it to recover them as sung, say, 150 years earlier? Common prudence might suggest the former, but modern editions of the literary texts are usually based on sources of the verbal text alone, which may be much earlier and preserve versions radically different from those of the musical sources, both in content and as to literals. Modern editors have often married such a text to a surviving melody without comment. Ideally however the musicologist will not simply take such a text and use it, but will apply the same principles to his own source, which though it may not have primary value for the text editor is, naturally, primary for the musical-textual entity which is the song itself. But it is not easy to decide when a text in such circumstances positively requires emendation; and a collaborator may not be prepared to commit himself.

Apart from necessary emendations, it is of course possible and in some respects highly desirable to make changes for the sake of legibility and ease of pronunciation. I would resist actual respelling here wherever possible: an editorial explanation of phonological values and the discreet use of diacritic signs is

---

[24] It is surprising how often hypermetric syllables, supposedly elided in reading, are given a separate note in musical settings. This is particularly true of late medieval versions of plainsong hymns; but it also occurs, for example, in secular song.

preferable. Nor should one convert the Middle English 'runic' signs (3, þ, and ð), except for the *wynn* (ƿ), which is too easily confused with *p*. But abbreviations should be expanded, either silently or by using italics for the restored letters; *u* and *v* should be given their modern values, and the long *i* eliminated except where it has the force of the modern *j*. Majuscules should be retained (or substituted) for the beginnings of pieces and sentences, and in proper names, but *not* for the beginnings of lines of verse (it is confusing and unnecessary). If they occur elsewhere, they should be silently replaced by minuscule.[25]

Medieval punctuation is usually too inconsistent and confusing, at least in musical sources, to be worth preserving. The editor should substitute the minimum of modernized punctuation necessary to preserve sense. He will also have to separate all syllables, a process fraught with complexity. It may as well be done on medieval principles, which are purely phonological, though manuscripts only manage to reveal this intermittently. Latin presents particular problems, since medieval sources are frequently at odds with classical method (for example writing *Sanc-tus* where a Latinist will write *San-ctus*). It is best to provide a prefatory explanation to avoid critical reprisal! Otherwise follow classical principles, which any good Grammar will reveal. Simply stated, these are that consonants should fall at the beginning of syllables, to the extent that a syllable may begin with any combination of consonants which can begin a Latin (or Latinized Greek) word. Compound words, however, are divided into their components (the *Liber Usualis* even prints *pot-ens*). This method can lead to phonological absurdity (*red-emptor, o-mnis*, etc.), but at least it is consistent.

I am myself opposed to the modern notion of including several syllables under a group of notes united by a cross-beam. Its claims for increased legibility seem to me exaggerated, and it is after all a very recent innovation: singers of opera and oratorio coped for centuries with the complex rhythms of recitative,

[25] Old French requires accentuation on the following principle: the acute accent (only) is used, and that solely 'to distinguish the full vowel *e* from the corresponding feminine sound: it is used only in words of more than one syllable' (F. Whitehead, ed., *La Chanson de Roland*, which see for many other points of detail). The only other signs required are the diaeresis, cedilla, and apostrophe, the last to represent an omitted letter in the normal way. In Provençal texts, the medial point is used to indicate an omission from the *following* word, a practice which is beginning to find favour for Old French too. See also *Romania*, lii (1926), pp. 244-6.

written in the traditional way, without complaint. (Incidentally, the following convention for a triplet sign over separate symbols, e.g. $\overline{}^{3}$ ♪ ♪, will obviate confusion with the sign for a ligature.) But it is, admittedly, a matter of taste.

The second and following stanzas of a song may be underlaid to the music; but this is not normally found in the sources, and the attempt to underlay a large number of stanzas can lead to illegibility as well as multiplying editorial problems. Composers did not always consider the meaning and versification of the second and subsequent stanzas, and the resulting difficulties are often capable of more than one solution.

Ideally, all underlaid text, except for the most familiar items such as the Ordinary of the Mass, would appear in an appendix in prose or verse as appropriate, and with a translation into modern English. This, incidentally, is a good opportunity for providing the text with its own critical commentary. Considerations of space often impede the realization of the ideal, however. A useful convention with strophic song is to print the entire poem after a single underlaid stanza. For most purposes, it is pointless to provide a singing translation, though monophonic song could provide an exception to this; but a plain prose translation is an essential aid to intelligent performance, and at this level is a very much more useful adjunct than a glossary.

The actual underlay of the text may well present difficulties in some styles, particularly melismatic polyphony. The manuscript reading is of course the ultimate authority, but there are various reasons why it may not be an entirely reliable one. The text may be missing, or deficient, in some or all voices; and the underlay may be subject to various distortions, sometimes as a result of the scribe's having copied in the text before the notes. This can lead to a (not quite) 'constant' error whereby the syllables of the text repeatedly occur too soon in relation to the notes. In purely syllabic passages, of course, the opposite may occur. It is the editor's duty to decide whether any one part is actually to be sung, and, if it is, to allocate the syllables as correctly as possible under the notes.[26] It is not sufficient, even

[26] Editorial additions to the verbal text of the source should be given in italics or square brackets. The possibilities of partial texting in performance should not be overlooked: instrumental doubling, or resort to vocalization, can enable significant melodic ideas to be 'picked out' by texting. Repetition of words is virtually unknown before 1450; it should not be prescribed editorially until then, and only very sparingly and exceptionally before 1500 (*c*. 1540 in England).

in an edition of a single source, to supply the text exactly as it stands in the manuscript. A facsimile will do that job better. The editor must decide what 'constant' correction, if any, is needed, and may note substantive alterations in the commentary after taking such a 'constant' into account. He may decide, for example, to adjust the last syllable in any musical phrase to its last note, though I am far from saying that this is likely to be a justifiable procedure. As for noting variant underlay between the sources, this is a question which can only be decided by the editor on the basis of his knowledge of the materials. Variant underlay in a commentary is not likely to be consulted by a performer; the scholar who interests himself in such matters is unlikely to get a clear picture from a commentary and will need to consult originals or photographs. Several recent volumes of *Early English Church Music* offer examples of a method of indicating such variants, however. Attention may be drawn to cases of difficulty by means of a footnote or special sign in the score.

The study of existing editions of medieval music will teach one more than the fullest verbal explanations. Older editors, as we have seen, often clung to a literalistic presentation which, however accurate, made for difficulties in reading. Much of the credit for the establishment of today's methods belongs to Apel, whose epoch-making *Notation of Polyphonic Music* introduced the secrets of medieval notation to a new generation of readers, taking into account the needs of English-speaking students for the first time. In his editions, and those of Schrade and Bukofzer, the foundations of modern Anglo-American editorial practice were laid. If it has been possible to suggest an occasional refinement, it is because the foundations are so solid.

3

Renaissance Music

The period covered by this chapter is from about 1450 to 1600; but the principles already put forward are still largely applicable, especially to the earlier part of the period, while the recommendations of the present chapter are, in some respects, applicable to music in Renaissance style written after 1600.

The topics will be discussed in the same order in this chapter as in the previous one, in so far as they remain relevant. The special problems of keyboard and lute music will be dealt with at the end. Owing to its closer approach to the modern system, the notation of Renaissance music in general calls for less elaborate editorial procedures than does that of the Middle Ages. To a large extent they amount to a simplification. The discussions that follow are self-sufficient as far as possible; but a reading of the previous chapter will reveal in some cases the principles on which the recommendations of this one are based.

The reduction of time-values is still a major issue for music of this period. Modern practice varies widely. The old collected editions of Obrecht and Josquin, as we have seen, employed original note-values with little if any impediment to legibility; but English music of the same period has normally been edited in quartered values, a practice extended by some editors to music written as late as *c*. 1555; and indeed some editors of Giovanni Gabrieli and Monteverdi quarter even their values in triple time. For my own part, I am content to see Continental music from 1450 to 1520 transcribed in halved values: this reduces the risk of notational paradoxes in complex proportions. Nor do halved values do any harm in conventionally written Renaissance polyphony up to 1580 at least, but they can be a nuisance in such contexts as *note nere* madrigals or in highly ornamented idioms, whether vocal or instrumental (there is little merit in substituting modern hemidemisemiquavers for Renaissance demisemiquavers). A decision in problematic cases may well be based on the need for consistency throughout the works of a single composer or the contents of a particular manuscript. Where the arguments are evenly balanced, I would always opt for original values. (For the consequences of reduction on the editorial beaming of the smaller note-values, see above, p. 25; see also below, p. 71).

English music is a rather special case: the quartered values nowadays almost universally applied to music of the early Tudor period throw its structure into better relief, though I would not myself carry that method beyond the end of the Henrician period except for a few pieces written in a rhythmically archaic fashion. Since a good deal of music written after about 1560 is best transcribed in original values, the lifespan of the 'halved-value' method is rather short. But it fits most of the music of the late Henrician, Edwardian, and Marian periods rather well nevertheless.

The situation is complicated by the exigencies of a decaying proportional and mensural system, and by the rise of *tactus* theory in the fifteenth century. From about 1450 onwards most 'normal' duple-time music is written not in C but in ₵. This has the effect of transferring the *tactus* (defined as an upward and downward movement of the hand and corresponding roughly to two beats for a modern conductor) from the semi-breve to the breve; but only a slight increase of speed (if any) is intended. It is music in this mensuration whose time-values we have been discussing. This means that C, in such a context, implies augmentation. When it occurs as the mensuration of a complete piece, as it does for example in certain archaic survivals of the later fifteenth century, in the *note nere* madrigals of Rore, and in certain types of late sixteenth-century English music, it is to be read simply as an alternative time signature. For the first and third of these categories, it need not affect editorial policy; for *note nere* madrigals however, it inhibits the use of halved values even if these are used in ₵, since its effect is already to make the crotchet the main unit instead of the minim.

In passing it may be noted that the signs ₵ and ☉, which around the middle of the fifteenth century came to signify augmentation, imply double augmentation in the context of ₵, i.e. a fourfold increase in value whereby the minim is regarded as a *tactus* equivalent to the breve. They are used with this meaning, for example, in certain works of Obrecht, in which ₵ represents normality. Later still they acquire a vaguer meaning denoting some kind of triple time.

Triple time in the later fifteenth century was often written in

Φ rather than O, perhaps by analogy with ¢ for C, and as part of a general tendency to combat the slower speeds implied by *integer valor* notation. Pragmatic considerations sometimes reveal a relationship between Φ and ¢ (for example in the Eton Choirbook) similar to that proposed for O and ¢ in the previous chapter.[1] In this mensuration the *tactus* is in theory thrown on to the perfect breve, though in practice the consequence is merely that a sign formerly indicating double speed is now used to indicate normal or slightly faster speed. An imperfect breve *tactus*, on the other hand, is usually designated by O2, when an additional halving of its values will normally be appropriate.[2]

After 1450, however, and to an even greater extent from 1500 onwards, triple time was often indicated not by perfect mensuration (whether or not affected by diminution) but by the application of *sesquialtera* ($\frac{3}{2}$) or, more rarely, *tripla* ($\frac{3}{1}$) proportion. These were thought of in relation to the basic mensuration of the piece, which was normally ¢ rather than C. The signs conventionally used for these two proportions were many and various, and are fraught with ambiguity. When they are used simultaneously with the basic mensuration there is no difficulty about the interpretation; but generally they are found in successive sections of a piece, though occasionally a bar or so of 'overlap' provides the clue to the interpretation.

Whatever the correct interpretation in individual instances, the effect of this use of *sesquialtera* and *tripla* proportion was to increase the speed of triple-time music in relation to that of duple, whereas formerly the reverse had generally been the case. Thus editors now often find it convenient to provide an additional halving of values in triple time, in relation to their policy for duple time, and even (where duple-time values are unreduced) to quarter them. These procedures have indeed been pursued into the early Baroque period: the merits and demerits of doing this are discussed in the next chapter. So far

[1] Above, p. 17, and Ex. 2, p. 24.
[2] For O2 see the Offertorium of Ockeghem's *Requiem* (*Collected Works*, ed. D. Plamenac, ii, p. 92 and Plate XIII); Busnois, Mass *O crux lignum*, Gloria at 'Qui tollis' (*Cw*, cxxiii, p. 8), in contradistinction to Φ, e.g. at Sanctus 'Osanna' (ibid., p. 25), where a faster tempo is implied. The sign O2 in effect denoted *modus maior* with imperfect *maximodus* — hence the later use of C2, C3, O2, O3 to indicate various combinations of *modus* and *maximodus* (see Morley, Thomas, *A Plaine and Easie Introduction to Practicall Musicke*, London, 1597, p. 13; repr. Farnborough, 1971; ed. R. Alec Harman, London, 1952, pp. 23-4). Both Ockeghem (Mass *L'Homme armé*) and Busnois in the work cited use ⊙ and ℭ as signs of augmentation.

as Renaissance music is concerned, the result will often be a gain in legibility and in consistency of notational style, though I feel that the difficulties created by retaining the larger values can be exaggerated.

Hand in hand with the question of note-values goes that of barring and the means of notating it. By far the bulk of Renaissance music is unbarred in the sources (the special problems of keyboard and lute music will be discussed at the end of this chapter). As with later medieval music, barring should neither conflict with nor be dictated by *tactus* theory. The choice of bar-length has as great a bearing on legibility, and on the suggestion of appropriate character and tempo, as the choice of note-values. The most frequent situation to be found, of course, is music with the breve *tactus* notated in ¢. Here the bar-length will normally be that of the *tactus* itself. But late sixteenth-century music, transcribed in unreduced values and slower in tempo, will often require barring by the semibreve, whether the signature is ¢ or C. In triple time, the most suitable bar-length will often be at variance with *tactus* theory: its choice must be based on the editor's feeling for the pulse of the music.[3]

It is understood that the barring of Renaissance vocal and instrumental polyphony is editorial, and no special notation (such as broken lines) is needed to suggest this. My own preference is for unbroken bar-lines through the whole score: this corresponds to such Renaissance precedent as exists, and no one nowadays supposes that tied notes are any more than a method of making up the arithmetical total of the equivalent in Renaissance notation. To draw the bar-lines just through the individual staves tends to reduce the capacity of barring to assist co-ordination and to point to underlying metre, though groups of staves can be marked off in this way to indicate polychoral groupings (see Appendix III, where various acceptable alternatives are also shown).

Laying aside such eccentricities as 'isochronous' layout, with

---

[3] The animadversions of Van Crevel in his editions of Masses by Obrecht imply an equation of bar-line and *tactus* by previous editors, though there is no evidence that they thought specifically in these terms. The recommendations in S. Rubio, *Classical Polyphony* (Oxford, 1972), fall into the same trap; in general, Rubio's observations as to mensuration are applicable only to the later sixteenth century. H. K. Andrews, *Introduction to the Technique of Palestrina* (London, 1958) has a valuable summary.

or without ticks above the score to indicate the *tactus*,[4] there remains one widely used method of barring of comparatively recent introduction, known as *Mensurstrich*. In this, the metrical divisions are marked between the staves only. The advantage of *Mensurstrich* is that the rhythmic independence of the individual voice-parts is preserved, and editorial ties can be kept to a minimum. The disadvantages are that the metrical structure of the music leaps less clearly to the eye, and that singers tend to get lost when counting the longer values. But the rigours of the method have been mitigated by a recent convention which permits the use of the tie at line-ends: this is preferable to the older compromise which inserted, small and in round brackets, the *remaining* value of any note still subsisting at the beginning of the new line.[5] Editors who use *Mensurstrich* also usually indicate prolongation of final syllables of words to the end of the period for which a long note is in force (as opposed to the moment at which the final notational symbol of the phrase to which it is sung occurs), though this (if expressed with the usual horizontal line) tends to aggravate the confusion with staff lines and ligatures inherent in the practice. Legibility would be considerably improved if all notes longer than the (modern) breve were written as tied notes.

Another criticism of *Mensurstrich*, that it cannot be used to express different bar-lengths in different voices, is not really valid, since the vertical strokes between the staves may be attached to those to which they apply without extending to an adjacent one.[6]

The choice of editorial time-signature depends, of course, on the length of bar chosen. This should follow sensible modern convention, care being taken to express the pulse of the music properly (e.g. not confusing $\frac{3}{2}$ with $\frac{6}{4}$). A double time-signature such as $\frac{3}{4}$ $\frac{6}{8}$ may be used to indicate a variable pulse; it should not be used for the haphazard changing of bar-lengths, which

[4] Used by Van Crevel in the editions cited. There are no barlines: the music occupies proportionately the same space as the time which it consumes.

[5] Clearly it is an advantage for the editor to send the publisher a score laid out exactly as for printing.

[6] See Busnois, Mass *O crux lignum*. A recent further compromise is to bar the individual staves only, substituting a small stroke above and below to accommodate notes which would otherwise have to be tied, e.g. . (Any note longer than the modern breve, however, is tied.) In many ways this is the most satisfactory method of all: see Ockeghem's 'Salve Regina', ed. J. Milsom (*Mapa Mundi*, B 5).

are better specifically indicated at the point of change. Avoid such things as 2, or ⸸.

Original signs of mensuration and proportion should not be shown on the staff. At the beginning of a work or movement, they will be indicated on the preliminary staves: subsequent changes should be shown above the staff in the score (and added in square brackets if missing in the source but understood by the editor). A very generally observed exception, however, consists of the retention of ₵ and C *when time-values are unreduced*, and this is unobjectionable.

The scale of reduction should be indicated, though it need not be shown for every piece if a uniform practice is followed throughout a publication. There is no need to repeat information given in the editorial commentary, provided this is adequate to cover all situations. It is a good practice to indicate the first note, or group of notes, in the preliminary staves;[7] but this is not always a sufficient substitute for indicating the scale of reduction, since such matters as ligatures, proportion, or coloration may affect the appearance of the original notation in a manner confusing to the performer and student. The best way of indicating the scale of reduction in a score is in the form ♩ = ◇ : i.e. the minim in transcription is equivalent to the semibreve of the original. The old-fashioned shape of the original notation prevents any confusion as to which is which. The policy should be to use the largest note-value (within the limits of the bar) which is not subject to change by virtue of the rules of mensuration; so it may be necessary to write ♩ = ♪ instead of the above. The equivalence should be in terms of the written appearance of the original notation, not of a hypothetical *integer valor*. The form ✕¼ is also usually unsatisfactory in Renaissance music since it begs the question as to whether the reference is or is not to *integer valor*. The only really safe method is to indicate the equivalence in visual terms and to indicate any departure from it in proportional passages.

As in later medieval music, it is important to indicate tempo relationships between sections which have a different mensuration. It is often valuable to suggest specific tempos, and these may be of help in supplementing a recommended tempo relationship. (The ways of showing this have been dealt with in Chapter 1; see also Ex. 2, p. 24.)

---

[7] For general comments on the use of preliminary staves, see above, p. 10.

In Renaissance music, page layout is likely to be of less significance in the apprehension of overall structure than it is in the case of medieval music. But it should not be neglected altogether, and the use of *Mensurstrich* will necessitate some forethought on the part of the editor, who should if possible provide the printer with a layout which can be reproduced as it stands. Consideration should also be given to the division of the music into sections. The principal portions of a Mass (Ordinary or Proper) should be regarded as separate movements and given fresh preliminary staves (if these are being used). Further breaking down into titled movements (such as Crucifixus, Qui tollis) is usually undesirable in Renaissance music, though this would not necessarily apply to the separate *partes* of a motet or madrigal. A normal, thin double bar-line will serve to mark off what the editor considers to be 'sections' within a 'movement', and the bar-numbering should be continuous (whether or not interrupted by plainsong insertions) from the beginning to the end of the movement.

If one or more voices are to be temporarily dropped from the score, it should be made quite clear which ones are to remain. (It is surprising how often this elementary point is overlooked.) Normally, voices should not be omitted other than for a complete section. The process does not necessitate fresh indentation for the new section, nor even a fresh start on a new line. The score can be reduced or enlarged by one or two voices at any point in mid-line provided that a double bar is ruled through the score; though if a larger difference is to occur it is best to arrange for this to coincide with a new line. In the latter case, abbreviated voice-names must be given above (or before) the staff; in the former case, even this is not necessary, nor are fresh clefs needed, unless a staff is being re-appropriated for a different voice.

This raises the question of consistent voice-naming and abbreviation. For Renaissance music, the best solution would seem to be to follow the naming of the principal source used, but for one reason or another this is not always possible or expedient. In much music written between 1450 and 1500, as for the previous period, only the Tenor and Contratenor parts are normally named in the sources. Contemporary literature suggests such names as Cantus, Discantus, and Superius for an unnamed top part, of which Cantus raises the minimum of preconceptions as to performing pitch. Two upper parts in the same range may be labelled 'Cantus Primus' and 'Cantus Secundus'.

Editorial voice-names of this kind should be placed in square brackets; but it is equally possible to substitute a new nomenclature altogether and to list the original names in the commentary. This is unlikely to be desirable for late fifteenth-century music in the chanson and chanson–motet styles, but it may well be appropriate for other types of Renaissance music. Latin names may be given in the vernacular, particularly if there is contemporary evidence of the vernacular equivalents (as there is, for example, in the case of English music of the late fifteenth century). The names of partbooks are not necessarily applicable to all the compositions within them, and there are even examples of labels being mixed up in the rebinding. It is best to retain standard designations if possible, but these may require prior explanation.

It is possible to designate parts by roman numerals, but even these are not devoid of ambiguity. Common sense would suggest that they be numbered from the top of the score downwards; but some scholars equate (e.g.) IV with Quadruplum, reading I as Tenor in thirteenth-century scores. Besides, parts having the same range, such as Tenor and Contratenor, do not readily admit of a logical numbering. If V, VI, etc. are used as abbreviations for Quintus, Sextus (as I recommend), neither they nor the 'first' four parts will be in the order of the score.

The commonest arrangements of part-names, with suggested abbreviations, are given in Appendix II. They are consistent, and easily comprehensible. It is important to note in the commentary any change from original nomenclature.

The order of voices in the score does not normally present difficulties in Renaissance music.[8] For a Tenor and Contratenor of the same range and written in the same clef, it will usually be appropriate (as for the previous period) to place the Contratenor above the Tenor, a useful guide being again the pitch of the final note. In double-choir and polychoral music, the voices of

---

[8] The main texted part of a chanson or other accompanied song should normally appear in the score in the place suggested by its compass (see for example certain chansons by Ockeghem and Busnois, and the 'consort songs' of Byrd and his contemporaries). The same applies to duets, dialogues, and the like, and to certain verse anthems, when what is notationally the 'same' part may be alternately vocal and instrumental. This principle should override preconceptions as to the appropriate position of a part-*name* in the score: so that we may have, for example, in Ockeghem's chanson 'Fors seulement', Tenor, [Cantus], Contratenor, in that order.

each choir will be grouped together, the order of the choirs being suggested by nomenclatures and (in the case of some Venetian polychoral music) by the range of the different choirs. (The allocation of individual voices to a specific choir is often a matter for musical analysis, since partbooks may contain no clue as to their intended distribution.) Melody instruments combined with voices are best placed in a group together; keyboard and lute accompaniments will naturally appear at the bottom.

Original clefs should be indicated, preferably on preliminary staves but failing that in the commentary. It is of particular value to show these, and the range of each part, in Renaissance music, as so many arguments about performing pitch and vocal colour rest upon this evidence (see above, p. 10).

Much as I regret the decline in musicianship which has led to unfamiliarity with the variety of clefs formerly in use, it would be unthinkable to retain them all in a modern edition. It is a curious paradox that one is more likely to find a variety of C clefs in scores of nineteenth- and twentieth-century music than in modern editions of 'early music', while the transpositions of a modern brass band score would throw the average score-reader of Renaissance music into a fit. A variety of clefs cannot be a serious impediment to a well-trained singer: indeed, I know singers who would rather perform from a Renaissance partbook than from anything a modern editor can produce. But there are demands of consistency as well as of nostalgia, and there is little point in admitting (say) alto (c'^3) and tenor (c'^4) clefs if all others (except f^4 and g'^2) are to be excluded. This would merely result in combinations of clefs uncharacteristic of Renaissance music. Continuity with practice appropriate to the medieval period demands that there should be no change without good reason. Altogether the arguments favour the use of only 𝄞 , 𝄢 , and 𝄞 in Renaissance vocal polyphony.

In instrumental consort music, nevertheless, there is much to be said for retaining the alto clef for middle parts of appropriate range. These are most likely to be played by string players, either on the viola itself or on the viol, the techniques of which they will most closely associate with the viola and its notation. The combination of treble, alto, and bass clefs is neither offensive nor unhistorical; it is easily read and is likely to have the widest general usefulness. It is probably best to reserve the tenor clef for high-lying passages in bass parts, though even here the alto may be used.[9]

The transposition of Renaissance music is a minefield. I do not want to enter into historical arguments here. Learned disquisitions about the absolute performing pitch of Renaissance music may be only partially relevant to an editor's decision. In the first place, most singers do not possess absolute pitch, and the few who do are probably happy enough to transpose their parts. Secondly, whatever scholars may say about pitch, differences of opinion remain, and a conductor might well have a different requirement for practical reasons. Finally, pitch is by no means standardized even today, and decisions based on the assumption that $a' = 440$ will not be of universal validity. If performers are going to have to transpose anyway, it may as well be from the original written pitch as from some figment of the editor's imagination.

Against these arguments, it can be pointed out that the needs of keyboard accompanists (whether required by the score and contemporary performing convention, or whether needed for rehearsal purposes only) have to be considered, and that their difficulties, especially in transposition by large intervals, can be considerable. It is also fallacious to suppose that there is any objective incorrectness in transposition to remote keys: it anticipates only very slightly the methods on which our modern major–minor system is based.[10] It is of course confusing if in the process of transposition the key-signature is modified as well (e.g. by transposing music in D minor without a flat to F minor with four rather than three flats), but even that merely throws

[9] The alto or tenor clefs should not normally be used in fifteenth-century chansons, whatever the views of the editor as to instrumental performance, particularly if the octave-transposed treble is also used. But the combination of C clefs and the transposed treble may be unavoidable in certain types of accompanied sixteenth-century vocal music; and as one will encounter this frequently enough in modern scores, it can hardly be regarded as objectionable. Indeed, the same part may have to change from one to the other according to its function (see preceding footnote).

[10] Sixteenth-century organists were themselves sometimes expected to transpose to remote keys: Schlick (*Spiegel*, 1511, ff. iii$^\text{v}$, iv$^\text{r}$) recommends *avoidance* of transpositions to D and E major, but Bermudo (*Declaración*, 1555) allowed keys as far afield as B and C minor in modes 1 and 2, giving key-signatures of three sharps and two flats respectively, and similarly distant transpositions of other modes. Morley (1597) refers to 'such shiftes [as] the Organistes are many times compelled to make for ease of the singers' (p. 156; ed. Harman, p. 261) in connection with music in C minor (two flats).

an additional responsibility on the editor to make the source-readings clear.

The real objection to transposition to remote keys is a psychological one: there is a danger that it may inculcate a romantic style of performance by creating factitious resemblances to inappropriate parallels. It also gives a misleading impression of scholarly exactitude in the matter of absoluteness of pitch.

There is however a certain amount of Renaissance polyphony which is written so far from a realistic performing pitch (by such Renaissance standards as existed as well as by our own) that some transposition is inevitable. The psychological disadvantages mentioned above are contained if transposition is limited to a 4th or a 5th. Even the interval of a tone is not inconsistent with the Renaissance practice of written transposition in relation to cantus firmi and modal structure. Nor do I entirely discount the possibility of remote transpositions; I simply feel that on balance their psychological impact outweighs their supposed exactness in terms of absolute pitch. Of course the direction of transposition affects the outcome, particularly if the original is in a 'remote' key by Renaissance standards: one might well transpose more readily from C minor to D minor than to B flat minor.[11]

The keyboard part in vocal and instrumental ensemble music requires special attention. Such parts begin to appear in late Renaissance sources and initially (and for longer in England) consist generally of an outline score on two staves. The editor must first decide whether such a part represents an outline for actual performance or is rather merely an *aide-mémoire* for a choirmaster. If the latter, it may be omitted altogether, except perhaps in a collected edition; if the former, it will probably require 'filling out', which may be done in small notes. It may also need transposition. Sometimes a keyboard or lute accompaniment actually conflicts with the parts which it nominally duplicates: this may be because it is an alternative (e.g. lute accompaniments in English solo songs which also exist in versions for four voices, or organ parts in English anthems which exist also in versions with instrumental consort accompaniment); the editor may print both in the same score as long as it is made

[11] On pitch and transposition generally see A. Mendel, 'Pitch in Western Music since 1500: A Re-examination', *AcM*, 1 (1978), 1–93 (with a very full bibliography).

clear that the versions are incompatible. Otherwise he should endeavour to assimilate them (and list his changes in the commentary). English verse anthems or services, and seventeenth-century 'consort suites', have independently conceived keyboard parts which normally present little difficulty, though even here the problems of incompatibility and incompleteness (especially in the 'full' sections of verse anthems) do arise. Another rather specialized problem is the duplication of solo vocal material in a keyboard accompaniment, for example in the solo madrigals of Luzzaschi or (to anticipate) certain movements of Monteverdi's Vespers. These are questions which need to be dealt with on their own merits as they arise.

An editor may add a keyboard part on his own account, either because he believes it to be desirable in performance (though missing in the sources) or for rehearsal purposes. Nowadays, however, there is little reason to provide for the latter function unless one is requested to do so by the publisher.

For the early part of this period, the editorial procedure suitable for medieval music may be followed with regard to key-signatures and accidentals.[12] As the period progresses, however, the method can be simplified in certain ways. Key-signatures begin to acquire more stability and are more readily distinguished in function from accidentals. The editor should not in my view modernize them (in the sense of adding or subtracting sharps or flats); nor, in ensemble music, should 'partial' signatures be edited out (though as in medieval scores they will still carry a modernized meaning in respect of octave-pitches). It is therefore desirable to retain, for the purpose of reflecting the difference in force between Renaissance and modern key-signatures, the use of small accidentals, in addition to purely editorial accidentals above the staff.

The validity of accidentals occurring in the course of the line gradually diminished during the Renaissance as they lost their potential of medieval times, and for much of the period it is safe to regard their force as continuing no further than the editorial bar (after which retention can be regarded as purely editorial). The point at which this happy state of affairs can be said to have been reached varies from place to place and from repertory to repertory. For all practical purposes line-ends can now be ignored; since key-signatures now rarely changed during

12 Above, pp. 29–33.

the course of a piece, both score and commentary can generally be disencumbered of these impedimenta. But with the continuing decrease in the validity of an accidental there arises an increase in the number of accidentals which in modern notation are redundant. Should these be retained in the score or not? The question is not an easy one to answer.

Renaissance convention, in fact, grew towards a system (partly achieved in late Renaissance music) whereby every note requiring an accidental (except, normally, for immediately repeated notes) was given one. Cancellations were not marked, except again for repeated notes (though here, unfortunately, practice is not wholly uniform). This system was also adopted in much Baroque music, including that of J. S. Bach; but by his time composers, copyists, and printers were moving towards the modern system.

Editors of J. S. Bach normally omit the 'superfluous' accidentals and mark cancellations within the bar with full-sized naturals. This may (and will) be criticized, but it can at least be said of this method that it converts one consistent system into another, and the one familiar to most performers of his music. But it will not do for late Renaissance music generally, since the sources as a whole are inconsistent in their approach and the possibilities for different interpretations are too great. What then are the alternatives?

Let us illustrate the possibilities by an example of a typical cadential phrase in the late sixteenth-century notation (Ex. 3, p. 58). The scribe (or printer) is in the habit of repeating accidentals within the phrase; but he has omitted a sharp at A, and also for both f's. There is no reasonable doubt that both f's need to be sharpened (though the first could just perhaps be left unsharpened if the following note is also natural); but there is reasonable doubt about the g' at A. The printer *may* have intended a natural simply by omitting the sharp, but his omission of sharps from both f's casts doubt on this. The harmonic context, of course, might well be a factor in making the decision.

We shall assume, for the sake of simplicity, that all editors will wish to sharpen both f's, and that they indicate editorial accidentals above the staff. They may or may not make the further distinction between 'editorial' and 'consequential' accidentals. Overleaf is shown a variety of editorial procedures, both with and without a sharpening at A.

Ex. 3. Example of cadential phrase in Renaissance notation

(i) editor opts for sharp at A   *(ii)* editor opts for natural at A

The first editor omits 'redundant' accidentals and boldly indicates an unmarked cancellation with a full-sized accidental. This is the method of most editors of Bach. It works if scribes are absolutely consistent over the whole range of music covered by the editor. That is a dubious proposition in the case of Bach, to say nothing of his contemporaries; it would be untrue of any but the tiniest samples of Renaissance music, other than tablatures. Within the editorial bar, it shows neither the absence in the source of a positive accidental, supposing the editor believes it necessary, nor the absence of a cancelling accidental, supposing he does not, except by noting such facts in the commentary. The potentially disagreeing performer is therefore left without relevant information, at least in the score itself.

The second method also omits 'redundant' accidentals, but regards an unindicated cancellation as 'consequential': 2(*b*) is clear, but 2(*a*) is not—has the editor assumed prolonged validity or has he left out a source accidental? The third method is a variant of this, but here the editor has intepreted cancellation within the bar, in 3(*b*), as a purely editorial decision, or at least as one not to be distinguished from a consequential one. The performer does not know if the editorial natural cancels a source sharp or merely reflects its absence; 3(*a*) has the same ambiguity as 2(*a*).

The fourth method is one that has occasionally been adopted, for example by Hilda Andrews in her edition of My Ladye Nevells Booke. It is unambiguous, but it is inconsistent with modern notation and involves an unnecessary number of 'editorial' accidentals: 4(*a*) means that the source does not have a sharp at A, but that the editor considers it necessary, and that it does have a sharp at B; 4(*b*) means that the source does not have an accidental at A (unless there is a footnote to that effect), nor a cancellation, but that the editor considers the cancellation desirable, and has indicated it as a (supposedly editorial) one. The method would be preferable if it were to distinguish between editorial and consequential accidentals; but, even so, it is illogical in 4(*a*) to provide an additional sign where there is none in the source, and to suppress one where there is.

Method 5 attempts to reproduce the source exactly, except for the addition of bar-lines, though even these would be present in keyboard scores. Taking the accidental as applying only to the note immediately preceding it, the sharp at A in 5(*a*) is properly considered to be editorial. At the same place in 5(*b*), the cancellation is indicated either by silence or by the presence of a purely cautionary natural in brackets. The great disadvantage of this method is simply that it is too imperfectly understood to be workable. Only with the very liberal addition of cautionary accidentals for cancellation could it be regarded as practicable.

Method 6 is unambiguous, and is not incompatible with modern practice. Accidentals are considered to have their modern significance, but the resulting 'redundant' ones are simply retained. If the editor decides on cancellation at A, he interprets this as a consequence of the non-repetition in the source; if he decides on retention he does nothing, though he might well add a cautionary sharp in round brackets.

The obvious objection to this method is that it involves an element of 'overkill'; accidentals are granted their modern force, but 'superfluous' ones are nevertheless retained. Yet other methods, of which the ones most commonly used are those represented by methods 2 and 3, are ambiguous to an extent that calls into question the whole principle of presenting the evidence to the performer in the score itself. Although still not common practice, method 6 has been gaining ground for many years now[13] and is recommended for scholarly editions of specialist repertories.

The alternative is to provide the information in the commentary in connection with method 2. If, however, the convention of the source is to mark virtually all the required accidentals, a further possibility is for the editor, having described that convention in sufficient detail, to indicate in the commentary those places within the editorial bar in which a repeated accidental, though assumed by the editor and required by the normal procedures of the source, is missing. In practice this will only work if the convention is the one just described (p. 57), and is adhered to fairly consistently (for the treatment appropriate for lute and certain types of keyboard tablature see below, pp. 64–5, 66, and Appendix IV). Incidentally, either the 'positive' or the 'negative' treatment of 'redundant' accidentals in the commentary may be denoted by a special symbol, such as α and β respectively; but unless the incidence of such mentions is very large, the space saved will be minimal. A phrase such as 'accidental' (or 'no accidental') 'before 5th note' is usually all that is required.

It sometimes happens, particularly where sixteenth-century English music is concerned, that an editor wishes to omit accidentals, even if they are present in his sole or primary source, on the grounds that they were added at a relatively late stage in the transmission of the music and do not reflect the composer's intentions. In such cases it is desirable to signal such omissions, either in a footnote with or without reference to the commentary, or by means of a special sign such as the small circle used by Paul Doe in his recent edition of Tye's Masses (*EECM*, xxiv).

Ligatures and coloration should be shown in the usual manner. The simplified methods of Renaissance notation in these respects scarcely call for comment, but one may note in passing the frequent use of *minor color* (e.g. ♦♩ which usually means ♩. ♪ rather than a triplet). *Color* is also used to clarify part-writing, as well as in almost all proportional passages, in early Tudor keyboard music. The omission of ligatures deprives performers of important negative evidence as to word-underlay and articulation, and is to be deprecated. Even when sources

---

[13] E.g. G. Cavazzoni, *Orgelwerke*, ed. O. Mischiati, 2 vols. (Mainz: B. Schott's Söhne, 1959–61).

conflict, and even when satisfactory underlay cannot be achieved without breaking ligatures, those of the primary source should be given. The editorial tie will not normally be needed in ensemble writing of this period, but if it is, the usual sign ⌒ should be used.

Alternating plainsong, transcribed from a suitable source, should always be included when necessary. The methods previously described will serve for the most part. In English pre-Reformation music, the usual interpretation of the *plica* or 'strene note' in a cantus firmus suggests that it should normally be regarded as a simple prolongation of the main note, whatever the intended meaning originally; but this is not always the case, and of course the interpretation in polyphony need not necessarily reflect contemporary monophonic performing practice. Transcriptions of syllabic chant in late medieval and Renaissance versions ought to distinguish between the square and the diamond-shaped *punctum*, as this may have a bearing on the rhythm. One can think of various ways of doing this, but a simple method is simply to write diamond-shaped notes (in place of round ones) on the staff. I cannot say that I have ever seen this done. The use of diamond-shaped notes in the *climacus* is covered by instructions previously given, but an editor who considered them to be of rhythmic significance could always emphasize their presence in the same way. Other differences of note-shape (principally that between *virga* and square *punctum*) appear to have no rhythmic significance.

The cantus firmus in polyphonic works is sometimes presented in a form of notation resembling that of plainsong. The usual equivalences are: ꞁ = ▢ , ▪ or ꞁ = ◇, ♦ = ♩. The notes may also be dotted. This notation must of course be brought into line with that of the other voices, and the equivalences explained in the commentary. Occasionally, in English music, whole compositions are written in this or a similar way.

In collected editions, cantus firmi and other *cantus prius facti* should be quoted complete from a suitable source in an appendix, for analytical purposes, and identified, wherever possible, in the commentary.

Lacunae should be dealt with in the manner suggested for medieval music.[14] As always, there is a distinction to be drawn

[14] Above, p. 40.

between omissions by the scribe, damage to the source, and the expansion of abbreviations.

The presentation of the verbal text is as much a problem for editors of Renaissance as of medieval music. In one respect it is more so, for there is the vexed question as to whether to modernize the spelling of the text. From about 1500, in the development of most European vernaculars, modernization ceases to be a real distortion of language, though it can still obscure the evidence for phonological differences between sixteenth-century and present-day speech. It also makes the transcription of certain archaisms difficult. Traditionally, editorial practice has varied from one language to another. French editors of their vernacular settings have usually adhered to sixteenth-century orthography, like their editors of text. In England, conversely, the long tradition of modernizing Shakespeare and his contemporaries has been reflected in musical editorial practices: recent *Musica Britannica* volumes of medieval and Renaissance carols have carried modernized texts, as did the older editions by Fellowes of madrigals and songs.

This can be defended in part on the grounds that singers do not normally attempt anything approaching contemporary pronunciation (though there have been some interesting experiments), and that in any case this is only partly reflected in the orthography of those times. It can also be maintained that it is less essential when the texts have been separately edited on rigorous principles (as have those of the English carols). But the editors of English 'madrigal' verse have themselves employed modernization on the grounds that spelling in the musical sources varies so much from one part to another that a truly authentic version cannot be obtained from them.[15] (In much the same way, editors of Shakespeare maintain that the spelling of the sources is not his own in any case, that the vagaries of Elizabethan spelling are pure 'accidents' of the language, and that nothing is to be gained by offering 'old spelling' for its own sake.)[16] On this argument, it seems to be the musical edition itself which provides the best context for preserving the old

[15] *English Madrigal Verse*, ed. E. H. Fellowes (Oxford, 1920; 3rd edn., ed. F. W. Sternfeld and David Greer, Oxford, 1967).

[16] For a recent attempt at modernization, with an explanation of the difficulties encountered, see the edition of the plays of Ben Jonson by G. A. Wilkes, 4 vols. (Oxford, 1981-).

spelling, since it can retain distinctions between one voice-part and another.

My own view is that sixteenth-century orthography offers no great difficulty to the performer, provided that certain conventions, pure tricks of typography in most cases, are changed. *U* and *v*, *i* and *j* should be changed in accordance with their modern values. (Editors should beware: a form such as *proud* could mean 'prov'd'.) The letter *y*, used as the equivalent of the thorn (þ) by sixteenth-century English printers, should be changed to *th* (e.g. *the* for *ye*, and *that* for $\frac{t}{y}$). Abbreviations, in any case, should be silently expanded. It may be necessary to modify punctuation| and capital letters and to provide apostrophes in accordance with modern usage. Text repetitions, indicated by signs such as ·*//.*, are of course written out in full, though they may be marked by ⟨angle⟩ brackets, with italic type or square brackets for purely editorial supplementation. Latin orthography presents fewer difficulties, since classical principles were revived at the Renaissance. That of the sources (whether medieval or Renaissance in character) should be preserved, except for the rationalization of *u* and *v*. *J* may be preserved for consonantal *i* if desired, since this is still currently in use as a standard orthography. An editor may of course wish to recommend a specific system of pronunciation, be it standard Roman ecclesiastical Latin or some national variant (see, e.g., *The Byrd Edition*, iv, ed. P. Brett; there is a survey of the whole topic by F. W. Brittain, *Latin in Church*, 2nd edn., Alcuin Club, 1951).

Renaissance composers were less likely to set a distorted version of a poem or other text than their medieval predecessors, but the version of a musical source, unless it is plainly impossible, may nevertheless be preferred to that of a literary source if it seems to be what the composer actually set. As in the Middle Ages, the second and subsequent stanzas of a strophic song were sometimes ignored by the composer in the details of his setting and may not be worth underlaying. If they are to be printed as verse after the music it will save unnecessary duplication in the commentary if the first stanza is prefixed in the same way. All underlaid text should be given separately, either in this way or in the commentary, and a translation given where appropriate.

Underlay is likely to present fewer difficulties than in medieval music, though in some repertories, such as Anglican service music, problems may remain (see above, pp. 43–4). Word-division is more likely to correspond to that of modern Grammars, which should be followed unless the source gives clear evidence of a contrary system (see above, p. 42).

Special considerations apply to the transcription of keyboard and lute music. English keyboard music up to about 1560 is still quasi-medieval in its notation, particularly with regard to accidentals, to which the methods appropriate for medieval music should be applied. 'Partial' key-signatures are, however, impracticable and should be edited out. Barring is usually haphazard (if present at all) and is best ignored. Scribes some- times ruled a page with vertical lines in advance and simply squeezed into them as much music as they could fit; later scribes then drew crooked lines to rectify imperfect co-ordination between the staves. It is scarcely feasible to retain such features in a modern edition.

Some editors feel that in keyboard writing the indication of editorial accidentals above or below the staff is impracticable. This is not necessarily so, but of course it will sometimes happen (mostly in later music) that the middle note of a chord requires alteration, and also that the layout of the parts inhibits the placing of accidentals between the staves. One way to overcome this is simply to name the note to which the accidental applies (e.g. 'F' above the stave—the octave-pitch will be obvious), but this looks inelegant. On the other hand, the distinction between editorial and consequential accidentals remains important, and there are serious difficulties about a solution which presents both types as small accidentals before the note. Square brackets around the purely editorial ones is a possible and to my mind perfectly satisfactory solution.

In some Continental two-stave keyboard repertories, neverthe- less, a tablature-like system of notating accidentals is employed which permits much simpler editorial procedures. In this, every note requiring chromatic inflection is marked with a dot.[17] The system is usually so consistently managed that it is satisfactory to use method 1 of those mentioned earlier in Ex. 3: omit 'redundant' accidentals and mark cancellations within the bar (i.e. notes without a dot on their second or a subsequent appear-

[17] Apel (1953), pp. 4, 6. Attaingnant mixes dots, sharps (rarely), and flats.

ance) with a full-sized accidental. Editorial accidentals should be put in square brackets. The commentary records mistaken accidentals, mistaken omissions after their first appearance in any bar, and any instances of actual cancellation in the source.

This method is also found in some of the many Continental sources of keyboard music which are written in open score. In others, moreover (in both closed and open score), conventional accidentals are employed with such consistency that method 1 can be adopted. The decision to do so must be based partly on an appreciation of such things as the range of sources which the editor will wish to bring within a unified system, or the demands of a series.

German keyboard tablatures also offer a degree of consistency in regard to accidentals which is absent from most other types of source, and for these too, therefore, method 1 is appropriate. This applies not only to the letter-notation itself (in which the letter-shapes are modified to indicate a sharpening), but to the staff in the case of Old German Tablature, in which inflection is normally indicated by special signs. The sign nominally indicating D ♯ will of course usually mean E ♭ and should be so interpreted. Even in such tablatures, however, editorial accidentals are often required, especially in intabulations of vocal music.

Some types of tablature impose on the editor the responsibility of selecting a suitable key-signature. This is particularly true of sources written entirely in letters (New German Tablature) or in figures (Spanish Tablature, and its Neapolitan offshoot used by Valente), but it is not confined to them. In any system in which the notation of accidentals is in principle unambiguous, corners may be further cut by the application of a key-signature which reduces the necessity for accidentals in the line.[18]

Continental keyboard sources, whatever the notation, are usually barred with some regularity, and this can often be retained in a modern edition (see above, p. 38). But in other pieces, while the barring is regular, it nevertheless distorts the metrical structure of the music. This is particularly true of certain types of piece in a triple metre descended from the medieval *basse danse*, but barred in quadruple time in the source. The best solution is to alter the barring and to indicate the original by means of short vertical strokes above the staff.

[18] Missing accidentals catered for by the editorial key-signature require mention in the commentary.

Open score is of course normally to be reduced to two staves, and, even if method 1 is employed with regard to accidentals, each 'voice' should be made self-sufficient in this regard. Editors should not rule out the occasional 'migration' of a part from one staff to another, either for legibility or to indicate the disposition between the hands, provided that the part-writing is made clear by means of a continuous straight line between the staves. In most other types of keyboard notation there is an implied or explicit division between right hand and left, and the editor should retain this unless there are very good reasons for not doing so.

Time-values should not normally be reduced after about 1550, though they may be halved or even quartered before that. However, the equivalences between German rhythmic signs and those of ordinary mensural notation are not exactly as they may seem, and Table VI shows these for some representative sources of the period. In general, transcriptions from such sources demand special discussion of this point in the commentary.

Lute music has its own special problems and characteristics. Time-values (which may be reduced in an edition) are not normally ambiguous. Barring is usually regular, but may be too frequent for comfort in transcription. The notation of accidentals is inherent in the finger-placement system (though editorial accidentals are often required nevertheless), and method 1 is appropriate. A suitable key-signature may be supplied. But more fundamental issues remain.

The pitch of solo lute music is purely relative, and transcription into staff notation is inevitably a distortion. But lute transcriptions from mensural sources, and lute accompaniment to song (or in other contexts embodying staff notation) usually reveal that the sixth course of the standard Renaissance instrument is to be thought of as *G*. If the result on this assumption leads to an improbably remote key, then the sixth course may be taken as *A*. Evidence for either can be found in contemporary documents. But there is a sense in which no key, however remote, could be said to be objectively incorrect.

Ideally, any edition of lute music would be accompanied by a transcription of the original tablature for practical use, though to obviate frequent page-turns it should not be printed in score with the staff notation. The editor may also offer a facsimile either in addition or as an alternative to a newly printed tabla-

Table VI. *Mensural equivalents in old German keyboard tablatures*

Name of note		Longa	Brevis	Semibrevis	Minima	Semi-minima	Fusela	Semi-fusela
Mensural notation								
Buxheim (*c.* 1470)[1]	Staff							
	Letters							
Virdung (1511)[2]	Staff							
	Letters							
Schlick (1512)[3]	Staff							
	Letters							
Kotter (1513-32)[4]	Staff							
	Letters							
Kleber (1520-24)[5]	Staff							
	Letters							

[1] Munich, Bayerische Staatsbibl., Cim. 352b (*olim* Mus. 3725), known as the *Buxheimer Orgelbuch*. This notation is a refinement of those in earlier tablatures. There are variants in all MSS in the treatment of *longa* and *brevis*.

[2] S. Virdung, *Musica getutscht und aussgezogen* (Basel, 1511). Facsimile ed. Schrade (1931), and *DM*, I, xxxi. So also the Latin, French, and Flemish versions.

[3] A. Schlick, *Tablaturen etlicher Lobgesang und Lidlein uff die Orgeln und Lauten* (Mainz, 1512). Ed. G. Harms (Klecken, 1924, rev. 2/1957), and R. Walter, *A. Schlick, Orgelkompositionen* (Mainz, 1970). Facsimile, Leipzig, 1977.

[4] Basel, Universitätsbibl., F. IX. 22, also known as the Amerbach Codex. This notation in Kotter's table, but the MS itself uses the notation of Kleber (except for black *longa*): so also Basel F. IX. 58, also written by Kotter.

[5] Berlin, Staatsbibl., Mus. ms. 40026. So also all other German tablatures up to 1551 (Hans Buchner, Basel F. I. 8a), with only minor variations in the treatment of the *longa*.

ture, or he may refer instead to an existing facsimile. But none of this can absolve him from the obligation of providing as rigorous a transcription into staff notation as circumstances will allow. The principal remaining problem, once those of pitch and time-values have been solved, is that of polyphonic interpretation.

Lute tablature indicates only the starting-point of each note, and it is possible for a transcription to reproduce only this information. In some pieces—preludial and rhapsodic works without polyphonic interest—this is all that is required. In such cases, transcription on to a single staff (with the clef 𝄞) will suffice. But in most works there is at least an element of polyphony. On the lute, the sound of an open string does not disappear immediately unless it is stopped in order to produce another note; and a stopped string will resound briefly unless it is re-stopped at another point or the finger is removed for other duties. The retention of the finger to prolong a sound is specifically indicated in some sources, but it was doubtless a normal part of good technique. The re-use of a finger limits the extent to which literal prolongation is possible, but it is generally accepted that an editor may legitimately go beyond that point in indicating the polyphonic structure of the music. (Ideally this should be done by a tied note in square brackets.)[19] For this purpose, two staves and the use of treble and bass clefs are normally necessary. Rests, being inherently editorial, do not require small print or other special signs; but they should be limited to what is essential for clarity.

It is clear that the editor must have a good working knowledge of lute technique to be able to perform this task satisfactorily. It is also desirable to indicate the use of higher positions of the hand when this is not dictated (in chords) by necessity.[20] Right-hand fingering, the use of a divided course, and the specific indication of prolongation are other occasional features of lute notation which, as they have a bearing on the resulting sound, require a complement in staff notation. The study of a really fine edition (such as Gombosi's of the Capirola Lutebook)[21] will teach much more than can be intimated here.

[19] See *The Collected Lute Music of John Dowland*, ed. Diana Poulton and Basil Lam (3rd edn., London: Faber, 1981).

[20] For a method, see *An Anthology of English Lute Music*, ed. David Lumsden (London: Schott & Co., 1954).

[21] *Compositione di Meser Vincenzo Capirola*, ed. Otto Gombosi (Neuilly-sur-Seine: Société de musique d'autrefois, 1955).

4
Baroque and Classical Music

In editing the music of comparatively recent times the difficulties are considerably lessened, but the temptation will perhaps be to assume too readily that the solution to various problems lies on the surface. The topics will be dealt with in this chapter in much the same way as in those preceding; but while to a large extent the treatment will be (as previously) self-sufficient, a reading of those chapters will help in understanding the background to some of the problems discussed. Occasionally, specific reference will be made to the discussion of minor matters which do not require renewed attention in this chapter.

The reduction of time-values ceases to be a major issue in the editing of Baroque and Classical music. In some early Baroque music in triple time it may be thought desirable to halve or even quarter the note-values to improve legibility and to counter the impression which they give of an unduly slow tempo. This is not necessarily inadvisable, provided that the scale of reduction is indicated and a suitable tempo relationship with adjacent duple-time music is suggested. But some composers, in particular Frescobaldi, used a wide range of time-values in triple time, precisely in order to indicate tempo, and it is a pity to spoil their notational picture. Moreover, the difficulties of reading music with a semibreve beat are often exaggerated. Editors of later music, even of much later music, have sometimes been tempted to reduce time-values,[1] but this is unwarranted. Our present-day methods are directly descended from those of the Baroque, and then as now a very wide range of note-values was available to suggest different styles.

Nevertheless, early Baroque music does exhibit some archaic notational features, of which some, though not all, are better abandoned. Ligatures and coloration are still sometimes found: these should be represented by the conventional signs already referred to (above, pp. 38–9), not retained in their original form.

---

[1] Somewhat exceptional instances occur in editions of organ sonatas by Mendelssohn, ed. Sir Ivor Atkins, and Rheinberger, ed. Harvey Grace (both Novello).

The old form of the crotchet (from which, incidentally, its English name derives), both separately ♩ and in groups joined by a cross-beam ♫♫♫ , is sometimes found, even as late as François Couperin. It need not necessarily be preserved, though it has been by some editors,[2] who have thus been able to retain the original beaming.

Early Baroque barring still sometimes conflicts with metrical structure and may be replaced by a system which reflects the structure more faithfully.[3] In partbooks barring may still be absent altogether, in which case it should be supplied on principles applicable to Renaissance music. But for the most part Baroque music is barred in the sources in a manner which exhibits its metre with some faithfulness. Barring is prone to minor irregularities, especially in the early part of the period, and a line-end may or may not be intended to indicate the end of a bar. It is usually convenient to substitute completely regular and unambiguous barring, and the editor will have to decide whether to do this silently or to indicate his modifications in the score. A dotted bar-line will indicate an editorial addition; or one may adopt the more elegant procedure of Thurston Dart, particularly in keyboard music, which was to represent original bar-lines by drawing them right through the score, while those added editorially were drawn just through the individual staff. A bar-line omitted by the editor may be indicated above the score by a short vertical stroke, though care must be taken to distinguish between its use in this context and in that of the complete re-barring of a work.

If original time-values and barring are retained, original time-signatures should be kept too. In much Baroque music they retain a residual proportional significance which, if other aspects of the notation are preserved, can be of help to the interpreter. For example, in Frescobaldi, $\frac{12}{8}$ means (e.g.) twelve quavers in the time of eight, which may or may not be the equivalent of our own $\frac{12}{8}$; and it may well be cancelled by $\frac{8}{12}$. The fact that the use of archaic signs of mensuration and proportion is often inexact, or is made only partly relevant by the demands of rubato

---

[2] F. Couperin, ed. Brahms and Chrysander (Augener); J.-J. Froberger, ed. H. Schott (Heugel).

[3] The original barring may be retained in the form of short vertical strokes above the system.

or tempo changes, is no reason for not placing the evidence of them under the eye of the performer. But if time-values have been reduced, or barring altered, the methods appropriate to Renaissance music must be applied, with a modernized signature placed in the score and the original above it.

Tempo indications should as far as possible be left as in the primary source. Additions to these, and editorial metronome marks, but not those tempo relationships which are implied by the notation, should be in square brackets.

The beaming together of quavers and shorter note-values is a scribal convenience originating in the fifteenth century, when it was applied to the hooked form of the crotchet (♩ in black notation) and smaller values. Its application to the crotchet is retained in the form ♫♫♫ in the Baroque. It cannot of course be preserved if that form of the crotchet has been edited out, but it is possible and often desirable to replace it by a slur or (preferably) by a ligature sign, with appropriate mention in the commentary. There is a good case for retaining the beaming of the source in quavers and smaller values in Baroque and Classical (and for that matter in some later Renaissance) music. Some early Baroque sources, however, do not employ beaming at all, in which case a modern method should normally be substituted, as it also should if reduced values have been substituted for the originals (see above, p. 25). Other sources employ beamed and unbeamed grouping haphazardly, in which case the frequent occurrence of separate quavers, semiquavers, and the like may be too disturbing to the reader to be reproduced. The main point, however, is that there is no half-way house in this matter. Either the beaming of the original is reproduced or (except by coincidence) it is not. All that can be said is that in the vast majority of cases it is worth considering very seriously whether the original beaming is not at least as effective and intelligible as a modern publisher's house style. In early notations it can be a way of indicating phrasing and can at least warn against incorrect phrasings, in a way that is often disguised by modern uniform practice.[4]

The present writer is not altogether happy about the modern substitution of beamed groupings for the separate symbols usually employed in the sources for the differentiation of

---

[4] Slurring and articulation are dealt with below, pp. 87-8.

syllables. But it must be admitted that the former is occasionally seen even in Baroque sources, and in such cases it should be retained unless it conflicts with editorial procedure in a wider context. If the source is inconsistent, it may be silently regularized, with only a general note in the commentary. The addition of editorial slurs to indicate syllable changes (except in short scores where the text is not fully underlaid) is to be deprecated. As late as Verdi, the slur was used to express legato in vocal music irrespective of syllable grouping.

There is a good deal to be said for retaining archaic notations such as ♩. ♫ to indicate a sharply dotted rhythm. If the interpretation is at all doubtful, it can be indicated above the staff in small notes, as it will in general have to be where rhythmic modifications are to be recommended.[5] In an ideal world, one would retain such pragmatic Baroque devices as the notation of ¹²⁄₈ ♩. ♩. ♩ ♪ ♩. by ¢ ♩ ♩ ♫ ♩; but the need to write a realization of the basso continuo may sometimes inhibit their preservation, at least when the composer has combined such a notation with the 'normal' method. In these cases the editor must provide a key to the original. Dots separated from their notes by the bar-line, the placing of long notes in the middle of a bar, and notes cut through by a bar-line call for silent modernization (though Brahms still used the first of these and it can be found in editions of his music in current use).

Some aspects of these latter problems call for reconsideration below in connection with the general topics of articulation, ornamentation, and rhythmic modification. In the meantime, however, it is necessary to consider the question of clefs, transposition, key-signatures, and accidentals.

The range of clefs employed in Baroque and Classical music is of course much narrower than in Renaissance music, though wider than that in current use. In particular the soprano clef (c'^1) was in general use for certain purposes until the late nineteenth century; but however much we may deplore its passing it is impracticable to retain it today (except in such specialized contexts as a pedagogical edition of *Die Kunst der Fuge*). But the alto clef is of course used for modern viola music, and the tenor clef for the tenor trombone and for the upper register in cello and bassoon music. There is no point in changing

---

[5] Below, p. 88.

these in a modern edition,[6] or in changing the numerous transpositions to which modern horn and trumpet players are, thank goodness, still well accustomed. Even if a publisher likes to issue *alternative* separate parts for (say) horn in F or trumpet in B flat, many players actually prefer the original transpositions, and they certainly look better in the score. The same goes for such things as the transpositions appropriate to oboe da caccia and oboe d'amore parts. But it has become the custom to 'de-transpose' timpani parts, and the analogous process in the horn and trumpet parts of Bach has the grandiose authority of the *Neue Bach-Ausgabe*.

The occasional use of an odd clef to indicate a transposition (e.g. ♮ for horn in G or ♮ for horn in D) should however be eliminated and the treble clef substituted. Here, as in all cases of clef-change or de-transposition, a preliminary staff should be used, showing the clef, key-signature, time-signature, and first note in their original form. (It is not necessary to do this uniformly down the score: only the staves which incorporate substantive changes require them.)

Baroque and Classical key-signatures, needless to say, carry their modern significance as to octave-pitches, in spite of the fact that some scribes (notably Bach) duplicate at the octave all possible pitches within the staff. The need for a special sign to indicate 'consequential' accidentals in this regard is therefore eliminated.

Baroque key-signatures, however, are often archaic in the sense that they do not correspond to the modern conventions for indicating the minor or major key of the music for which they are being used. Thus we have, e.g., one flat fewer or one sharp more for minor-key music (supposedly representing the Dorian mode and used as late as Haydn), and one flat more or one sharp fewer in major-key music ('Mixolydian' notation). It is a great mistake to modernize these. To do so adds to the difficulties with regard to accidentals, confuses the notation of a figured bass, and destroys the evidence for certain prevalent habits of thought in the area of tonality. The use of such key-

6 A possible exception would occur when a high-lying bass line doubles as the left hand of the realized figured bass. In such cases it might be thought desirable to use leger lines or change to the treble clef, though the separate part could still retain the tenor clef. It is as well to adopt the modern convention for cello music in the treble clef, i.e. sounding as written.

signatures is often, on purely pragmatic grounds, just as efficient as the modern equivalent. Moreover, there is no modern convention for the Phrygian mode, which frequently retains its individuality in Baroque music.

Occasionally it may appear that a wildly 'incorrect' key-signature (such as one flat for C minor) needs modernization; but on the whole it is best to leave well alone unless the omissions are a definite mistake leaving large quantities of necessary accidentals unmarked. In such a case, as an alternative to extensive editorial additions, one may repair the insufficiency in the key-signature. The additional accidentals should be noted as such either by means of a preliminary staff or in the commentary, but not bracketed or printed small in the score. In the vast majority of cases, however, this process will simply increase the number of 'redundant' accidentals (see below) and the need for 'consequential' cancellations.

We come now to the question of accidentals in the course of the staff. On the whole, two methods of procedure are in current general use. The first, which I will call the 'Bach' method since it is commonly employed by editors of Bach, simply translates Baroque notation into the modern equivalent.[7] Redundant accidentals are omitted, and any necessary cancellations within the bar, though they may not be marked as such in the original, are printed in full size. Any remaining purely editorial accidentals are dealt with in one of the following ways: above or below the staff; small, on the staff; in round or square brackets; or full-sized on the staff but noted in the commentary. All carry their modern force.

This method has several advantages. It is clear and consistent, and is applicable whatever has been done to the key-signature. It requires no complex instructions for the unscholarly user, and creates no doubts or ambiguities in his mind. It has already been recommended for certain categories of Renaissance music, notably tablatures. But it is less than ideal for sources and repertories which are inconsistent in respect to accidentals. Baroque notation represents a transition from the late Renaissance system (in which all notes requiring an accidental are given one, with the possible exception of immediate repetitions, and cancellations are unmarked) to the modern one. In such a pro-

---

[7] It corresponds to the first method described in the previous chapter.

cess of transition, many more instances of uncertainity may arise than can be accommodated by discussion in the commentary. Even with such a careful scribe as Bach himself, repetitions of accidentals within the bar, necessary by his criteria, are occasionally omitted. If the editor believes such an accidental to be necessary, he will simply omit the cancellation and say nothing. Yet he has, strictly speaking, supplied an accidental editorially. If the interpretation of such a passage is doubtful, it may be impossible to convey to the performer the extent of his choice (cf. Ex. 3 above, p. 58).

A great deal of Baroque music is notated somewhat haphazardly in this respect, and the occasional uncertainties in Bach's scores are as nothing compared with those in the sources generally. Modern editors have often adopted a solution (the second method in current widespread use) which identifies accidentals implied, but not stated in the source, by small print. However, the same device is often also used to indicate purely editorial accidentals; and 'redundant' accidentals are omitted (cf. method 2, p. 58 above).

In the vast majority of Baroque scores this method creates no serious difficulties, and it gives a truer picture of the source itself. But it contains the seeds of ambiguity. It is illogical to clarify what the source does not contain while remaining silent about what it does contain. Moreover, it fails to distinguish between consequential and purely editorial accidentals.

An unambiguous solution in appropriate cases would be to retain 'redundant' accidentals in the score and to distinguish clearly between consequential (or implied) and purely editorial accidentals.[8] The obvious objection, as already stated, is that it duplicates information unnecessarily for the performer, and may even confuse by creating the expectation of accidentals in contexts where the source does not specify them and modern convention does not need to supply them. Against this the following points may be made.

The method completely removes all possible grounds for doubt as to the reading of the source in individual cases. Moreover, the preservation of many 'redundant' accidentals would be a positive help to the modern performer, particularly in keyboard music. It leaves the editor free to decide in individual cases

---

[8] The sixth method, described above, p. 59.

whether unmarked but necessary cancellations within the bar are 'consequential' or 'purely editorial', according to the scribal habits of his source. But its great advantage is that it is applicable, without further complex explanations, to a wide variety of source material. As the modern system evolved, 'redundant' accidentals were reduced to a sprinkling of 'cautionary' accidentals which a modern editor might well wish to retain anyway. At the same time, cancellation within the bar came to necessitate specific signs, and their omission calls for 'purely editorial' supplementation; but the need for this is reduced almost to vanishing-point.

If 'consequential' accidentals are to be printed small, a different method is required for purely editorial ones. The method of showing them above or below the staff is apt to cause confusion when a figured bass is present. My own preference is for square brackets: this will not be found to be cumbersome in post-Renaissance music, where the need for such accidentals is usually very limited. Editorial cautionary accidentals will be in round brackets as heretofore. Incidentally, there is nothing to prevent a printer from engraving bracketed accidentals in small size, purely as a matter of typographical convenience.

In this writer's opinion, the inclusion of 'redundant' accidentals in the score does not violate the principles of modern notation (see Appendix IV) and is certainly the most convenient method for the editor. Ex. 4 shows two transcriptions of a passage from Bach's Flute Sonata in B minor BWV 1030 (first movement): 4(*a*) is according to the method just outlined, 4(*b*) after a standard modern edition.[9] But it is understandable that some editors and their publishing houses should prefer a score which contains only the essentials. The score from which Ex. 4(*b*) is taken, however, conforming to method 1 in the previous chapter, does not distinguish between cancellations actually marked by Bach, those which the editor has marked as a precautionary measure, and those which are required in modern notation but not in Bach's system; nor does the commentary enumerate the 'redundant' accidentals. It could be argued that in Bach's own scores

[9] Ex. 4 is transcribed from Berlin, Deutsches Staatsbibliothek, Mus. ms. Bach P 975 (facsimile ed. W. Neumann, Leipzig, n.d.); NBA, VI/3, p. 37. Both versions assume that the appoggiaturas do not require explanation at this point, and redistribute the music on the keyboard staves to reflect the part-writing. My edition adds suggestions for articulation and rejects the editorial accidentals at bars 55–6. The autograph is reproduced opposite.

Facsimile of J. S. Bach's autograph of Flute Sonata in B minor BWV 1030, extract from first movement (see Ex. 4, pp. 78-9)

Ex. 4. J.S. Bach, Flute Sonata in B minor BWV 1030,
extract from first movement

such refinements are unnecessary, since his intentions are usually
crystal clear; but that, even if unreservedly true of Bach himself,
is not necessarily so for other copyists of his music, let alone
the whole range of eighteenth-century scribes and printers.

The method represented by Ex. 4(*b*), therefore, would be considerably improved if the editor's own cautionary accidentals
were to be placed in round brackets, and consequential ac-

cidentals printed small, as already explained. Bach himself, however, notated the cancelling $e'\natural$ in bar 53, which is required in our
modern system (and which would have ranked as a 'consequential' accidental had he not done so), and the e'' and $g'\natural$ in bars
54 and 56, which although not strictly necessary are nevertheless
advisable. They would therefore remain in full size. Since the 'redundant' accidentals are too numerous to list positively in the

commentary, it is rather the omissions according to Bach's usual methods (which are essentially those of the late Renaissance — see pp. 57, 60) which should be listed. In the passage quoted there are none.

It is to be hoped that these explanations, complex though they may seem, describe methods which are straightforward in application and conform to sound scholarly principles. A summary of these, comprising an abstract of the methods recommended during this book, is given at Appendix IV.

We now consider the layout of the full score. Leaving aside for the moment the special considerations applicable to solo instrumental works, several points call for consideration. A source will consist of a score, separate parts, or both. While it is often tempting to retain the layout of an old score — and indeed it should not be altered without good reason — there are overwhelming advantages in standardizing the layout of orchestral scores according to the best modern practice: from the top down, woodwind, brass, percussion, voices, strings.[10] Paradoxically, a contemporary score of a seventeenth-century chamber work may need less modification than that of a nineteenth-century orchestral work. Even the retention of voice-parts immediately above the bass line is probably better avoided nowadays, though it has certain advantages in Baroque music and can still be seen in currently available miniature scores. The old-fashioned placing of horns above the bassoons should also be abandoned, except in wind quintets.

Old scores are often wasteful of staves, and it is frequently possible, and indeed advisable, to contract a pair of wind parts on to a single one. The symbols a 2 (both players), 1. (first only), and 2. (second only), if needed as a consequence of the contraction, should be added in round brackets. Stem direction and rests are essential tools for sorting out complex passages, but information should not be duplicated: one should not write, e.g.: a 2 ♩♩♩ . In Classical | orchestral | string | writing, the orthography of the source should be used and div. and unis. added in square brackets (unless they are original) to amplify its implications: thus one may legitimately have, e.g., [div.]♩♩♩. When a cello and a double bass part have been

---

[10] Solo vocal and instrumental parts lie above the strings except as noted in the following discussion.

contracted on to a single staff, one may specify Vc or Cb as appropriate in round brackets: if the original is itself on a single staff any original indications should be retained and editorial amplifications put in square brackets.[11] It must be admitted that Classical scores are not always models of clarity and it may not be easy to arrive at the precise intentions of the composer. For example, in the slow movement of his Piano Concerto in E flat K 482, Mozart's indications in the divided passages in bars 8-16, 41-3, and 153-6 suggest that the cello and double bass are to sound two octaves apart; but his intentions are more likely to have been that they sound in unison (see the careful discussion in the *Neue Ausgabe*, V/15, p. XVI). There is in any case an inherent ambiguity in the meaning of the word 'basso' in Classical times, while double bass players of those days, because of the restricted range and manoeuvrability of the instrument, would frequently have had to make modifications in performance. A conscientious editor will take a stand on such matters and offer a clear interpretation to the user.

Classical chamber music presents few problems of layout, but Baroque chamber and orchestral music calls for further comment. This will most frequently be edited from separate parts. Here the most important basic principle is to state clearly in the prefatory material what are the names of the original parts and how they correspond to the staves of the editorial score. This is particularly important with concertante material, and apropos the bass line generally. Baroque concerti grossi can often with advantage be presented on a reduced number of staves, with solo and ripieno parts sharing a staff between them. One problem here is that eighteenth-century parts often use terms such as 'tutti' and 'solo' (or 'soli') not to indicate the precise division of the material, which is inherent in the publication in separate parts, but to indicate its character to the individual player. The best solution is to retain all the original markings but to supplement them by abbreviated part-names (such as Rip, Conc), again in round brackets, to clarify the position when the staff contains only a single line of music.

The practical result of this can be seen in the reproduction of a page from an edition of the string concertos of John Stanley

---

[11] Round or angle brackets are in general suitable for indications which are implied by the original notation or layout but are not specifically marked in the source. See further below, p. 93, and Appendix I.

(Ex. 5, p. 84). Neither 'tutti' nor 'soli' correspond exactly to the requirements of the modern editor, so the abbreviated part names are added in round brackets where necessary. The editorial 'tutti' at the beginning, in square brackets, is deemed a sufficient indication that all are to play. The compressed score is a great deal easier to read than a printing *in extenso* would be, while the indications are precise enough to indicate to a conductor (and to the copyist of the parts) exactly who is to play what, and when.

The score also illustrates a method of dealing with the solo part in a keyboard concerto. Stanley's concertos were published in a form which made them playable as string concertos, keyboard concertos, or solo keyboard works. While it was comparatively rare to provide three versions of such a work, keyboard concertos were nearly always published, down to the end of the eighteenth century and even beyond, in a form which also allowed them to be played as solo keyboard works.[12] What they do not provide is a genuine written-out continuo part, such as a solo keyboard player was nevertheless normally expected to supply: the solo part in the tutti sections may even conflict with, where it does not merely duplicate, the accompaniment.

A possible way of presenting this material while providing a musicianly continuo realization for the tuttis is to use three staves, of which the outer ones correspond to the published keyboard part and the middle one (which can be engraved small and will in any case only carry small notes) represents a continuo part for the tuttis.[13] The part can be reduced to two (full-sized) staves in the solo sections. In the case of Stanley's concertos, however, the need to supply a continuo part for the string version leads to the use of three staves throughout. The outer

---

[12] Examples are provided by the organ concertos of Charles Wesley (of which a selection was published as his Op. 2), and the piano concertos of John Field (ed. F. Merrick, *MB*, xvii). But the autographs of Wesley's concertos demonstrate that the continuous solo part is a device of publication, not of composition. Some publications of Classical concertos resorted to figured bass in the tutti sections, a practice still observed in the published parts of Beethoven's First Piano Concerto Op. 15.

In this connection it is worth noting that the Baroque practice whereby soloists automatically played in tutti sections is probably valid for most Classical concertos up to about 1800. Mozart wrote 'col basso' in the piano part throughout the tutti sections in his piano concertos, and a comparable convention operated in most of the string and wind concertos. But the slavish doubling of the first violin part in a work like his clarinet concerto (published posthumously, autograph lost) need not be taken literally.

[13] See T. A. Arne, Concertos Nos. 1-6, ed. R. Langley (*MC*, lxxxi-lxxxvi).

parts represent the unaccompanied keyboard version, whilst the two lower ones are used for the string concerto version.[14] If the work is to be given as a solo keyboard concerto, it is necessary for the player's right hand to move from the lower to the upper staff, and vice versa, as indicated by the arrows.

In Baroque keyboard concertos the continuo function of the soloist is an integral element of the part, which should be placed at the bottom of the score. In Classical concertos, expecially if there are wind parts, it is probably best to place it above the strings, even if the editor decides to supply it with a residual (if optional) continuo function. But precise circumstances will differ: the solution for J. C. Bach may not be the best one for Mozart. Other solo parts in concertos should appear immediately above the strings, except that Baroque solo cello parts may be better placed above the ripieno bass line.

This discussion of keyboard parts leads us to the more general issue of continuo realization and its place in the score. There may be an occasional good reason for not realizing an essential keyboard continuo part in the full score of a Baroque or Classical work, and indeed many miniature and other scores in current general use adopt this practice. There is of course room for some difference of opinion as to how essential a keyboard accompaniment actually is. It is always possible for a publisher to provide a separate continuo part which does not appear in the score, and on the whole this is the best solution in Classical music, where the keyboard can either be omitted without real detriment or (as in Italian opera) may be alternately essential and non-essential. In Baroque music, however, it is usually more convenient to add it to the score; and if page-turns are not too frequent and the score is full-sized, it will not be necessary to provide a separate part as well: the continuo player, like the conductor (whose function he may in any case duplicate) can use the score itself. In Baroque chamber music, the provision of a musicianly and stylistically appropriate keyboard part is an essential prerequisite, and the player of course uses the full score.

It is usually practicable and desirable to retain the composer's bass line as the left hand of the keyboard part. If not, then the latter must appear on small staves below the score.[15] The right-

---

14 For this purpose some left-hand passages have to be marked '[continuo tacet]'.

15 This of course does not apply to keyboard concertos, in which the keyboard part itself provides a continuous bass.

Ex. 5. Stanley, Concerto Op. 2 No. 1 (extract from first movement)

*See Notes on Performance

hand part should in any case appear as a small staff. It is always possible to make the left hand more idiomatic, and for it to share in the formation of the chords, by printing small notes on the staff which carries the original bass line. Original figuring, which in the sources usually appears above the staff, should be placed below; it should also be included, for practical and educational reasons, in the separate bass part to which it is applicable.

Baroque string concertos, and certain other kinds of work, often supply two sets of figures, one for the solo violoncello or viola da gamba, and one for the ripieno bass. Whatever this may be thought to imply in terms of performing practice, it is usually impracticable and a waste of time and resources to write two different keyboard parts. If the solo and ripieno parts are conflated on to a single staff as previously suggested, this will usually make a satisfactory continuous left-hand part (differences in the figuring in tutti passages are usually trivial and can almost always be accommodated in the score or, failing that, in the commentary). If the conflation is impracticable, either a completely separate keyboard part will be needed, or else the left-hand part in the solo sections can be accommodated in small notes on the ripieno staff. Trio sonatas often have a separate bass line for the keyboard (the actual nomenclature, of course, is very varied and is a matter for study in itself): rather than conflate the two, it is perhaps best to keep them separate and add the keyboard right hand above the lower one. A similar layout often occurs in orchestral works, such as the autograph concerto scores of J. S. Bach, where a similar solution should obtain.

Individual works will inevitably present special problems which this brief survey cannot cover. Monteverdi's printed *bassus generalis* parts often duplicate material from the instrumental (and vocal) parts on two or more staves; it is better to supply a proper accompaniment and to note in the commentary variants between the *bassus generalis* and the separate parts. Works such as Vivaldi's *L'Estro armonico* concertos are almost *sui generis*; one should avoid making scores such as Einstein's of Op. 3 No. 11, in which the two viola parts of the original publication, which duplicate each other exactly from beginning to end, are solemnly reproduced in full. To put the matter in the form of a generalization: the exigencies of publication in separate parts of a set of concertos may often disguise the innate conception of an individual work, which it is the editor's duty to realize in his score.

The provision of a continuo part in Baroque chamber music, and particularly in continuo-accompanied solo music, may often necessitate, as previously indicated, the assimilation of the rhythmic notation of the bass line to that of the upper part or parts (see above, p. 72). Incidentally, the useful recent convention of notating an editorial continuo right-hand part on a small staff makes it impossible to retain the older convention of printing the instrumental melodic parts small. The newer method is more satisfactory from every point of view.

The actual style of continuo realization is not a matter that can be fully entered into here. But it is a mistake to write in something so uniquely personal that it impinges on the composer's prerogative. A good continuo part can often make something of an inferior piece of music, but in general anonymity is a virtue. It is often necessary to write a part which can be played equally well on the organ or the harpsichord (or indeed for that matter the piano, since whatever may be said about the practice Baroque chamber music will continue to be accompanied on that instrument for teaching purposes and in the home for the foreseeable future). As for the organ, its historical role in continuo accompaniment is immense, and should never be ignored. A somewhat neutral style is therefore inevitable; but a good player will embellish what he sees according to circumstances, and the best will play directly from the bass line.

A number of points of detail may now be considered. The reproduction of original dynamics, articulation, and so forth often causes difficulty. The most straightforward way of dealing with dynamics, as with other verbal indications, is to reproduce

them exactly as in the source, either in roman or in the bold
italic conventionally used nowadays, using square brackets for
the editor's additions (small type is insufficiently clear in this
context). And while it is a pity to respell or otherwise modify
such choice indications as Matthew Locke's 'lowder by degrees',
editors understandably fight shy of retaining such idioms as
'for:', 'pia:' and 'All$^{\circ \cdot}$'. It is good scholarly practice to expand
abbreviations; and in Baroque music this may legitimately be
extended to dynamic signs as well. Otherwise, and more particularly in Classical music, one may reduce all dynamic signs,
to the conventional 'f', 'p', etc., and to employ such standard
abbreviations as 'cresc.', 'rit.', etc. without comment.

Rather more important than the orthography of such signs is
their correct placing. Care should be taken, for example, with
the Classical use of 'fp', the constituent dynamics of which are
often spaced out under specific notes.[16] Dynamics sometimes
indicate points of structure, and care should be taken to avoid
moving them on spurious editorial grounds or supplementing
them in a way which robs them of their significance.[17] The
spacing of the constituent syllables (or even letters) in the word
'crescendo', and others like it, should be rigorously observed if
it is of any significance.

These problems apply equally to other signs and symbols.
The exact physiognomy of early 'hairpin' signs need not be
reproduced, but their placing must be as accurate as possible.
Unfortunately, in late eighteenth- and early nineteenth-century
music, the short diminuendo hairpin is identical in appearance
with the accent sign, especially in manuscript sources. Ultimately,
of course, this stems from the fact that an accent implies a
diminuendo; but it would be quixotic to print anything other
than a conventional accent sign when that is all that is intended.
The editor has to take a stand on such a matter, in which his
knowledge of the conventions appertaining to particular sources
and styles will play an important part.

A similar point arises in connection with signs of articulation.

---

16 A good example of this occurs at the very opening of the 'Prague' Symphony,
in which Mozart's minim 'f' tied to a crotchet 'p' was not printed correctly, so far as
I am aware, until Kroyer's Eulenburg score. See also the very careful edition by
Roger Hellyer of Mozart's Serenade in E flat K375 (*MC*, lxxv).

17 A blatant recent example occurs in the Kyrie of Bach's B minor Mass in the
Neue Bach-Ausgabe, where Bach's 'forte' in bar 48, marking the return of the ritor-
nello, has been supplemented by the editor in the viola part three bars earlier.

Slurs in Baroque and Classical music are often ambiguously placed, and the editor must again make firm decisions, recording any substantial ambiguities (and the basis of his procedures) in the commentary. There is of course room for scholarly disagreement on the precise implications of early slurring for different instruments, as well as for the voice. A note on performance may well need to refer to the question of articulation in general.

The usual eighteenth-century sign for staccato is the vertical stroke or wedge; and it is best to retain this, using the dot only if it is in the source, when its meaning may well be different. The characteristic Baroque articulation ⌢⌢ does not imply staccato at all. To switch to a supposed modern convention creates more ambiguities than it resolves.

The same must emphatically be said of ornament signs, attempts to tamper with which only lead to chaos. The pages of musicology, from Saint-Saëns to Dart, are littered with the debris of such efforts. It is singularly unfortunate that so many educational textbooks still teach an antiquated interpretation and naming of ornaments and articulations which never had much foundation in reality, though there are signs that a much needed change is on the way. There is no substitute for the original orthography and a full editorial explanation, together with, where possible and appropriate, a closely relevant contemporary table of ornaments. The notation of appoggiaturas, long and short, should remain unchanged, though it is better always to substitute ♪ for ♪ (which is only an eighteenth-century way of writing a semiquaver, small or large).

However thorough an editorial note may be, there will nearly always be a need to explain some ornaments by means of an interpretation above the staff. The same method will also serve to clarify an editor's recommendations as to rhythmic interpretation. Normally the note-shapes without the staff will suffice, though occasionally the latter will be needed. To employ a staff without good reason increases expense unnecessarily. It will however sometimes be desirable to write an editorial cadenza above the single note (or group of notes) for which it is a substitute; less frequently, an editor may justifiably embellish a whole movement in this way, though on the whole it is better to expound general principles and let the player devise his own realization.

Conventions for repeats and for first- and second-time bars

may be silently modernized, though there are some complexities. The multiple repeats of some Baroque music are often better left in the form of the original directions (e.g. for the *petite reprise*). There is of course no objection to retaining picturesque terminology (e.g. 'play $\begin{smallmatrix} c \\ y \end{smallmatrix}$ last strain twice') provided that the intention is clear. Even in the late eighteenth century, double bars and dots could be used in a somewhat cavalier fashion; analysis should be employed to test the authenticity of repeat signs (or their lack), and an attempt made to understand the rationale of the source's convention, if any such can be deduced.

Stem direction is another convention which may be silently modernized. Forms such as $\mathcal{N}$ should be avoided. When two parts are contracted on to a single staff, the stemming is necessarily editorial. Other aspects of this topic concern specifically the keyboard and other solo instruments.

Solo instrumental writing creates its own problems. The original distribution of the music on to two staves, in the case of keyboard music, does not always correspond to a practicable division between the hands. Attempts to regularize this can lead to awkwardness, and the convention is by no means uniformly applied even in more modern piano music. The modernization of clefs, however, may in some contexts suggest a redistribution, and it would be pedantic to rule this out. Publishers of solo keyboard music, after all, can have recourse to a facsimile edition if the desire is to retain precisely the original visual image. Nevertheless, the tendency today is to reproduce as closely as practicable the 'literals' of early keyboard music, and, with certain reservations, this is to be encouraged. Original 'beaming', for instance, can very well be retained, except where the original lacks it entirely.[18] Stemming, on the other hand, is best standardized: in manuscripts it is often chaotic, and the modernization of clefs can render it meaningless. The provision of separate stems for each note of a chord, as in the autographs of J. S. Bach and reproduced by all his best editors, is hardly necessary but conveys a pleasing sense of style. In general, the choice between separate or single stems (i.e. $\frac{1}{4}$ or $\frac{1}{4}$) in freely contrapuntal music is a difficult one (as is that of stem direction where one part falls silent); but the original orthography may suggest a suitable style even if it cannot be reproduced exactly. 'Missing' rests

[18] Above, p. 71.

may be supplied unobtrusively in small print, but this should be done sparingly, and only to resolve a potential ambiguity. It is not necessary to supply full rests for each and every contrapuntal part.

The editing of organ music poses some extra problems. Baroque organ music, even with pedal obbligato, was normally written on two staves; but it will usually be desirable to expand this to three. Some of the repertory (for example a great deal of Buxtehude's music) is written in tablature, which apart from the question of legibility can cause difficulties as to the length of notes and the distribution of parts. Indications for the use of pedal may well be haphazard, and indeed the editor should satisfy himself that the use of the pedals is actually intended. All editions of Buxtehude to date print a number of his works with a pedal part which is not so marked in the sources. While this may be justified in some cases, editors should not use a third staff for a pedal part that is neither indicated in the sources nor an inevitable consequence of the style. This is particularly true of cantus firmus voices in inner or upper parts, when the editorial indication of 4′ or 2′ stops makes the score unusable for other interpretations of equal validity.[19] In such cases the two-stave score should be retained, with or without editorial suggestions as to methods of performance.

The reduction of open-score sources (and indeed of tablatures) to two staves necessitates a clear notation to indicate when an individual part moves from one editorial staff to another, as it may well do in order to indicate hand distribution or to avoid unnecessary leger lines. On the other hand, the *apparent* part-writing of tablature sometimes disguises a contrapuntal texture: the transcription should reveal this, and it may be impracticable to indicate all the divergences from the tablature (which itself may well be a transcription from an original in staff notation).

The above discussion has assumed that the clefs used will be restricted to treble and bass; but for some editorial purposes (such as specialist collected editions) it may be thought advisable to employ at least the alto clef, in particular for the inner parts of certain types of organ music. It was so employed in scholarly

---

[19] In this respect, H. J. Moser's edition of Scheidt's organ music in *DDT*, i, is superior to the later edition by C. Mahrenholz. Incidentally, wide stretches in the lower staff may imply a short octave rather than the use of pedal, though the editor is at liberty to suggest the pedal as a solution to the problem of stretch. This must of course be clearly indicated as editorial.

editions of the nineteenth century, and is found even in the standard edition of the organ works of Brahms in current general use. For that matter, Mendelssohn sometimes uses four and even five staves in his organ sonatas (a feature again retained in the standard modern edition). S. S. Wesley also used four in at least one of his organ pieces; and certain French Baroque works requiring a different manual (or pedal) for each contrapuntal line cannot be properly edited otherwise. Nevertheless the general use of open score for contrapuntal keyboard works is probably a lost cause except for specifically educational editions.

Whatever system is employed for the treatment of accidentals, care should be taken, when two or more contrapuntal lines are on a single staff, to ensure that each is self-sufficient in that respect.

The wholesale duplication of dynamic marks in early pianoforte music can in most cases be silently dispensed with (with a note in the commentary to that effect); but any subtleties in the placing of dynamics, consequent upon such duplication, should be carefully retained.

Omitted bass lines in variation movements (which can occur also in continuo-accompanied solo chamber music) may be restored, either without any distinguishing mark, other than a general note in the commentary, or else within angle brackets (which require an explanation there).

Of other solo intruments, those employing finger-placement tablature require special consideration. The points made in the previous chapter remain valid.[20] The ideal solution is to print both the tablature and a transcription, which can and should of course embody a polyphonic interpretation when this is appropriate. In Baroque music the *style brisé* and unmeasured prelude present special problems in this respect, while such features as ornaments, the slur, doubled notes, strumming effects, and different tunings call for careful consideration. Normally two staves are required. Music for guitar and for lyra viol, on the other hand, is usually simple enough to require only a single staff with the clef 𝄞.

Other solo instruments call for little special comment, except for the use of scordatura (or special tuning) in the violin, viola, and cello. Since the object of scordatura is to help the player, it should be retained; but a transcription into sounding pitch should be added. Wholesale transpositions, such as those employed

[20] Above, pp. 66–8.

in Bach's Brandenburg Concerto No. 1 or Mozart's Sinfonia Concertante ᴋ 364/320d, are a different matter. There can be little objection to retaining the original written pitches in the score (though the more usual modern practice is to transpose them to sounding pitch); but in any case a publisher will ideally provide two separate parts, one transposed and the other not.

The presentation of vocal music of this period calls for little special comment. Clefs will normally be modernized. It is essential for the clef-sign used for the tenor part (𝄞) to be noted unambiguously in that (or some comparable) form. The notation of syllable change has been discussed above. In the text itself, word-division should follow an established convention. There will be less reason to modify the orthography than in earlier periods, but there may nevertheless be some justification for this, especially in English; and on the whole it is unlikely to distort the original significantly. In earlier texts, it may be necessary to regularize the use of *u* and *v*, *i* and *j*. In Latin, however, consonantal *j* may be retained even though its phonetic value is not that of the letter in English. There will normally be little reason to tamper with the orthography of Latin texts written in the seventeenth and eighteenth centuries, except for the regularization of *u* and *v*. Hebrew texts, needless to say, require transliteration, as do, for most purposes, any others not written in the Roman alphabet.[21] Foreign texts should be complemented by a prose translation.

Opera scores may well require clarification as to who is to sing what; and the provision of spoken dialogue, usually from a different source, is an essential feature of any work of which it forms a part. But the specific problems of large-scale vocal works, and of opera in particular, tend to require *ad hoc* solutions. Much depends on the purpose of the edition. At the same time, the publication of certain editions designed for specific performances is to be regretted. There is a great deal to be said for the publication of plain texts, innocent of transposition, re-scoring, and the like, on which an imaginative conductor can build. This need not exclude the provision of a continuo realization, suggestions above the staff as to vocal embellishment (including the performing conventions appropriate to

---

[21] For the transliteration of Russian, see *Hart's Rules*, pp. 120 and 131, and the references there given.

recitative), a singing translation, and other aids. Nor should scholarly standards be relaxed in 'vocal' scores (i.e. those with piano reduction of the orchestral accompaniment). A good vocal score of a Baroque work can often convey nearly as much as a full score (occasionally, as much), and it may in some cases be the most practicable form of publication.

We may conclude by noting some special considerations concerning the treatment of lacunae, errors, and variants in the music of this period. In general, lacunae, as previously noted, fall into three categories: those caused by damage to the source, accidental omissions by the scribe, and conventional omissions. Into the last category fall instrumental duplications of the type represented by such instructions as 'col basso', and the conventional omission of keyboard left-hand parts in the context of variation. These may be silently restored (in notes of full size) without comment, or, if the edition is to a very high standard of faithfulness, placed within round or, preferably, angle brackets. In either case any source directions become otiose and are omitted without comment.

An editorial continuo realization in a sense falls into the same category, but here the convention of printing it in small notes is so useful and well established that it should unquestionably be retained. Small print is also appropriate for reasonably extensive editorial reconstructions (whether of individual vocal or instrumental parts, or of whole sections of music); and small rests, as previously noted, may be added for the purposes of clarification. Short lacunae should be restored within square brackets, and a remark inserted in the commentary to indicate whether a missing note is 'om[itted]', 'illeg[ible]' or 'cut off' (e.g. by the binder).[22] Missing but recommended ornaments, dynamics, figures, and other signs should also be placed within square brackets, as small print is less readily distinguishable. Editorial slurs and ties are crossed through, while the treatment of missing accidentals has already been dealt with.[23]

The commentary is of course the place to note errors and variants. The method of doing this has already been discussed.[24] All but the most insignificant should be recorded, so far as the

---

[22] This method has the additional advantage of avoiding confusion with appoggiaturas and ornamental passages in small notes.

[23] Above, pp. 76-80.   [24] Above, pp. 8-10.

principal source is concerned; the readings of subsidiary sources may be represented fully or selectively, or ignored altogether, depending on the character of the source and its significance for the edition. The question sometimes arises as to whether the readings of subsidiary sources, particularly with regard to accidentals, dynamics, and ornaments, should be incorporated into the score and distinguished by such means as the use of small print, italics, and various kinds of brackets. In some cases, where two or more manuscripts or editions appear to have equal authority, there may be some justification for doing this. But on the whole it is better either to admit such material to the text or to treat it as purely editorial (see Chapter 1, footnote 10). The synoptic presentation of textual variants on a separate staff or system may be of value to the scholar but confusing to the performer. Typographical means may however be used on occasion to distinguish alterations made to a manuscript by the original or a subsequent scribe (either of whom might be the composer himself) or to a printed copy by hand. But to note extensive revisions by the composer will normally require the printing of a separate version.[25]

In sum, the editing of Baroque and Classical music, while not subject to as many pitfalls as the editing of earlier music, requires care and the consideration of innumerable topics of a minor but sometimes intractable nature. If a work is worth publishing (or republishing) at all, it will merit the most scrupulous attention to details of this sort.

---

[25] Some of the complexities involved, and the possible solutions, may be seen in two recent editions of Bach's Inventions and Sinfonias: that of the Neue Bach-Ausgabe, and the one published by Henle Verlag.

5

The Preparation of Copy

It is possible to take the greatest care over editorial methods and principles, and yet to neglect those aspects of presentation which can improve the chances of acceptance by a publisher and greatly speed the process of publication thereafter.

It goes without saying that a clear script is a desideratum. 'Good scribes use thick nibs and black ink', ran this book's predecessor, a recipe whose validity is amply confirmed by the late Thurston Dart's bold and characterful hand. The blacker the ink—and the whiter the paper—the clearer will be the result, and the better the photocopy you make of your manuscript. It is essential to keep an exact copy: your precious manuscript may have travelled half-way round the world before you see it returned with a first proof. Copies should also be kept of all proof stages—this writer speaks from bitter experience. Nothing can completely insulate one against loss in the post or in some other way, but the keeping of copies can greatly minimize the inconvenience thus caused and also enables queries to be dealt with quickly by telephone.

Modern editorial procedure involves the use of small staves, notes, and signs. It is difficult to make this clear in manuscript, and the convention has arisen of writing such notes and signs in red ink. This is perfectly acceptable (though it is advisable to give an explanatory note to the printer), but the difference in colour will not be clear in a photocopy. An alternative is to ring small items in red; a small staff such as is required for the right hand of a continuo part in any case requires such treatment.[1] This can be done on the photocopy as well, though if it has been feasible to distinguish small signs calligraphically some labour can be saved (but not on the copy sent to the printer).

An editor should of course study his publisher's house style (and the 'style within a style' appropriate to a specialized series) and as far as possible accommodate his demands to it. But this is not always feasible, and there can be flexibility where an

[1] The publisher may, however, undertake this and other tasks of copy-editing.

editor feels strongly about an aspect of notation which may be at variance with the normal style: for example in the matter of beaming, the drawing of bar-lines, or the conventions applicable to changed signatures. If necessary, he should issue instructions to 'follow copy' in various respects: otherwise, carefully laid plans may fail, either in the publisher's or the printer's office.

An editor may even (for example in medieval music) desire a printer to follow his own page-layout. If so, care should be taken to ensure that it is practicable. Normally, however, a printer will design the content of each page afresh. This will involve consequential changes in the incidence of clefs, key-signatures, and bar-numbers.[2] All this should be painless, though in practice certain misunderstandings can arise. It is impossible to anticipate every conceivable cause of ambiguity; but careful forethought will reduce it to a bare minimum, and any mishap can be corrected in proof. The nearer the editor can get to the printed appearance of the score, the simpler, quicker, and cheaper the whole operation will be.

Care should be taken with the writing in of texts in vocal music. It is essential to be clear and consistent in such matters as capitalization, punctuation, and word-division, for which *Hart's Rules* gives full guidance. (These rules do of course need a certain adaptation for this special purpose, and specific editorial situations may call for particular conventions; but they are an invaluable general guide and alert one to the problems of the most frequently used modern languages). The ideal method is to write in the texts clearly by hand in exactly the form in which they are to appear; failing a clear hand, they may be typed in. The use of undifferentiated capitals requires elaborate sub-editing, and, unless the editor does this himself, misunder-standings and errors will arise.

The exact placing of syllables under the notes should not be left to chance. One method is to place the *vowel* of each syllable below the appropriate note—another is to place its *first letter* below. Syllables should be separated by a hyphen, word-ends followed by a ground-level line (where the final syllable of a

---

[2] Bars (US: measures) should be numbered continuously through each 'movement' (as defined by the editor), placing the numbers at the left hand of each system for quick reference (though some editors prefer to number in fives or tens). Incomplete bars at the begining are ignored: first- and second-time bars are treated as alternatives (29*a* 29*b*, etc.). Provide continuous numbering when music abbreviated in the source (such as a da capo) has been written out *in extenso* as an aid to performance.

word corresponds to more than a single note-symbol), unless this feature is being designedly omitted.[3] Choral music may call for the sharing of a text between two parts or staves, in which case care should be taken to ensure that no ambiguity arises. The use of slurs or beaming (if either) to indicate syllabification should be consistent. Text should appear below the staff (except in short scores): in this context all dynamics and other indications appear above. When there is no text, tempo marks appear above, dynamics below.

A publisher will almost inevitably feel free to adapt headings and the like to house style, but a few general principles may be stated. An original title, when there is one, will frequently require modification: the preface should in any case make clear the various forms of title found in the sources, and the authority for the ascription to a composer. In general, a title should convey as concisely as possible exactly which work of a composer is being edited. Circumstances vary so much that it is impossible to lay down hard and fast rules, but ideally the first page of the music should convey all the information required for an unambiguous identification, irrespective of what may appear on the outer cover, in the preface, or in the notes. (In a collected edition, the possibility of making off-prints makes this highly desirable; the absence of a composer's name at the head of each piece in an edition devoted solely to his works can be rectified on the cover of an off-print. Such an edition may itself be the source of an authoritative means of identifying individual items, in which case the edition number at the head of the piece will be sufficient identification.) An original opus number (and 'number'), or the numbering of a standard catalogue or of a source-reference, when applicable, should appear, either as an adjunct to the title or (less logically) below the composer's name. This latter should appear on the right-hand side of the page in a full, standardized, authoritative form (obviously some variants are possible in some cases, but they should carry the weight of authority) with dates of birth and death.[4] The editor's name may appear at the left-hand side of the score, as in the

---

[3] See above, pp. 12, 49, for the special considerations applicable to Renaissance music.

[4] *The New Grove* is an obvious starting-point for establishing the appropriate form for the English-speaking world, and its conventions should be adhered to whenever possible.

first example below:

SOLO 9
Op. 4 No. 1

Edited by John Caldwell   John Stanley (1712-1786)

Other examples of titles are

LA SPAGNA

Josquin Desprez (*c*. 1440-1521)

MISSA CAPUT

Johannes Ockeghem (*c*. 1420-1497)

CONCERTO in D MINOR
BWV 1052

J. S. Bach (1685-1750)

SYMPHONY No. 3 in E♭ MAJOR, Op. 55

Ludwig van Beethoven (1770-1827)

It is not necessary to use capitals for titles: lower-case in a sufficiently bold type is an attractive alternative; or a mixture (as in the last example) may be used. Italics are best avoided except to indicate a distinction between English and foreign words. The title MISSA CAPUT could in fact appear in a variety of ways: Missa Caput, Mass 'Caput', Mass *Caput* or (in a volume devoted solely to Masses) simply as Caput.

An edition number, for instance in a collected edition of a composer's works, may appear either centrally above the title or at the left-hand side, in arabic and in a suitably bold type.

Headings of separate movements may legitimately appear in a variety of forms. In a Mass, for example, one may write simply (in italic) *Kyrie, Gloria, Credo, Sanctus, Agnus Dei* (rather than just *Agnus*) at the head of each movement, centrally. In an opera one might have (No.) 55. Recitativo; in a Classical symphony I, II, III, etc. at the head (centrally in each case). In Baroque and Classical music a useful alternative is to write, flush with the left-hand edge of the indented first system, e.g. 3. Sarabande; 1. Allegro; 2. Menuetto: Allegro. The last example illustrates the treatment of a movement's title with a tempo indication as well. The use of a numeral facilitates identification in the critical commentary.

In any event, there should be a clear correlation between separately titled movements and renewed bar-numbering. In certain multi-sectional works, particularly of the Baroque, difficult decisions may have to be made; but a clear system of reference is essential. End each 'movement', separately bar-numbered, with ‖, even if it ends with an imperfect cadence (one may write [attacca] editorially if necessary);[5] divide sections within movements by ‖ (this may be omitted for frequently-changing time-signatures, though not normally for key-signatures). For repeats within movements, of course, the conventions are :‖ :‖: ‖: (*not* :‖ etc. unless a reforming publisher cares to take the matter up).

The use of braces and brackets, and the layout of the score, have been dealt with in the preceding chapters. Several model score-layouts are given in Appendix III.

Dynamic and most other verbal instructions in the score (other than principal tempo indications) would normally be printed in italic without specific contrary instructions. If the editor requires roman type for original markings of this kind, or wishes to make a distinction between roman and italic, he must say so and underline for italic when required. This will obviate any possible misunderstanding.

The form and content of editorial letterpress has been discussed in Chapter 1. It should be typed on one side of the paper, with ample margins and double spacing. Footnotes should be kept to a minimum: they too should be double spaced and are best supplied on a separate sheet. All abbreviations (except for the commonest ones in general use) should be listed and explained. This applies to *RISM* and other sigla for libraries and sources, however familiar they may be to a coterie of specialists in the field,[6] and to abbreviations for time-values, parts, and pitches (with the possible exception of pitches in the system of Helmholtz, which is now standard: note-names, but not pitch-classes, should be underlined for italic).[7]

Hart's Rules is an invaluable aid to the achievement of

---

[5] This is a sound general rule, but there can always be exceptions where long-established practice and the authority of the composer suggest an alternative, as in the Passions of J. S. Bach.

[6] *The New Grove* has given one form of them a wider currency, but they are not easily remembered, and there is no point in sending users scurrying to the nearest copy.

[7] See Appendix I.

consistency in such matters as spelling, capitals, punctuation, and the like. The book also gives instructions for correcting proofs, which as far as letterpress is concerned is a straightforward matter. For the correction of music they require modification. It is sometimes necessary for the sake of clarity to write an alteration on the staff itself, in which case it should be ringed and a line drawn to connect the circle with the marginal sign for an omission or alteration. Every correction should be clearly linked to a marginal sign, whatever the method used to indicate it.

When reading music proofs it is advisable first to go through the music once, carefully, part by part, and then to check systematically for specific features: clefs, key-signatures, bar-lines (correct subdivision down the score, correct types of double bar, correct placing generally), accidentals, articulation, bass figures, and so on. The continuo realization should be checked for content (correct chords, avoidance of undesirable consecutives, etc.) as well as for typographical errors. One may then read through the score again, and, if possible, give it to a second person to read. All letterpress should be thoroughly checked.

The complexity of early music editing, and the occasional conflict with house style which it may produce, generally mean that at least two proof stages will be required. A publisher's reader will not necessarily be a specialist in the period, and may query legitimate editorial processes. Answer all queries intelligibly (*Hart's Rules*, pp. 33, 38). Music-setting may well be sent abroad: instructions and corrections should be indicated as clearly and simply as possible.

A knowledge of modern music-setting processes will help. Music is hardly ever 'engraved' in the technical sense nowadays, though the expression is still loosely used. Long before it died out, multiple copies were normally made photographically from a master printed directly from the engraved plate. With the development of photolithography, other technical aids, such as the stencil and the musical typewriter, have been developed. For the printer, they have the advantage that the work does not have to be done in a mirror image. In fact, they are quicker and cheaper in every way, and nowadays can be as elegant as fine engraving. Photolithography, moreover, enables copies to be taken from earlier editions made by whatever process; the original can be reduced or enlarged as desired, and corrections incorporated.

This book cannot enter fully into the business aspects of publishing early music. What has been said, nevertheless, implies a business relationship between editor and publisher. A publisher, it should be remembered, will himself have highly placed staff whose task is in the widest sense editorial; their responsibility is to accept or reject music for publication, and to ensure that what is accepted is published in conformity with their standards and style. A scholarly series may have (and ideally does have) its own general editor (or editorial committee) and style. Below this hierarchy comes the individual editor, who may either be commissioned to produce an edition or proffer his work unsolicited. A proposal for a large project may of course first appear in the form of a rough draft, and an editor of standing may be commissioned on the basis of his reputation alone; but in any event final acceptance will depend on the publisher's approval of the finished project. A small unsolicited project is on the whole best offered in finished form: there is the risk of rejection, but the edition can always be offered to another publisher.

Whether work is commissioned or not, the publisher may either offer a down-payment or a royalty. Royalty agreements are not so frequently entered into as in book-publishing, but an editor should consider whether such an agreement would not serve his interests better. The initial return may be small, but an editor has a right to benefit from the continuous sale of his work over the years. The publisher also has his interests, and he may refuse the payment of royalties. An editor should remember, too, that buoyant initial sales are not always followed by continued steady demand. The question of the agreement between the publisher and his editor is therefore a complex matter, in which the editor may or may not have an effective decision to make.

Another aspect of early music publishing, of concern to both publisher and editor, is the lack of any certain return from performing right. Both have a moral and a technical legal right to a return for the labour of making the music available for performance: but in practice this obligation is often evaded by performers, and it is difficult to prove that a particular modern edition of an early work has been used. In practice, therefore, most editors forego any expectation from this source (though there is always the occasional surprise); but it does make the publication of early music less commercially viable for a publisher, who can earn a great deal more from modern music and from questionable but distinctive arrangements of old music.

It should be remembered that a publisher retains a twenty-five-year copyright on the typographical layout of an edition, irrespective of the date and editorship of the music. It is in everyone's interest to observe this restriction on the photocopying of published material. In addition the publisher or editor (according to agreement) retains a copyright comparable to that of an author (i.e. until fifty years after his death) on his specific editorial contribution. This is harder to police, but it makes the copying, photographically or otherwise, of newly edited material illegal for that period, except for the photocopying of an unaltered facsimile. There are indeed certain exemptions,[8] but they do not embrace the wholesale photocopying of music for performance in any context.

Enough has been said to indicate that the financial rewards from publishing early music are at best unpredictable and at worst nugatory. For a large project of limited interest, indeed, it may be necessary for the editor himself to seek a subsidy. But no one who has read this far will be motivated primarily by a concern for profit. It will be enough if even a part of the expenses involved (which may be considerable) can be recovered. For the rest, there is a legitimate pride in the achievement of a work of genuine scholarship. To have contributed to the revival of the music of the past is its own reward.

[8] A leaflet giving guidance is available on request from OUP. A-R Editions operate an interesting 'copyright-sharing policy': for information write to A-R Editions Inc., 315 West Forham Street, Madison, Wisconsin 53703, USA. Their formula might well be considered by other publishers of early music in library editions.

Special Signs and Conventions

In the Score

Brackets:

[ ]   enclosed material is purely editorial (e.g. missing music except for substantial lacunae, missing verbal text if not in italic, missing accidentals if not in small type above or below the note, missing grace-notes and ornaments, missing dynamics and other verbal indications)

⟨ ⟩   enclosed material is indicated by special signs in the source but not fully written out (e.g. musical and verbal repetition, part-duplication)

( )   enclosed material is not in the source but is implied by its conventions (e.g. editorial cautionary accidentals — but not 'consequential' accidentals, which are printed small — and indications of part-distribution necessitated by editorial compression, such as Vc, Rip, a1, 1., etc.)

Small music type:

grace-notes, cadenzas, etc., written small in the original (not normally liable to confusion with the following uses; but a still smaller size is needed if employed in conjunction with the last three uses below)

editorial accidentals (if placed above or
   below note)   ⎫
'consequential' accidentals (if placed   ⎬   see Appendix IV
   before note)   ⎭

rests added editorially to clarify part-
   writing
substantial lacunae restored by editor   ⎫   on small staff
editorial interpretations above the staff   ⎬   where appropriate
continuo realization   ⎭

Italic type:

missing verbal text (if not in [ ])
coloured or otherwise visually distinguished verbal text (e.g. red text perhaps indicating solo performance in the original: necessitates [ ] for missing text)

Other signs

        ⌣   editorial tie or slur (in preference to the older dotted form)

   ⌐‾‾‾‾¬   ligature (also compound neume, archaic cross-beam)

⌐   ¬   coloration (see also p. 39 for other special signs)

⌐ – – – ¬   compound neume consisting of separate symbols

In the Commentary

For names of notes, use Helmholtz's notation in italics, as follows:

Pitch classes should be given in roman capital letters, e.g. clarinet in A.

Clefs and key-signatures: cite the clef by its letter-name and indicate the line on which it stands, counting from the bottom (by unanimous modern convention). For late Baroque and Classical music the formulae F^4, C^3, G^2 etc. will suffice. 'K-s 3 flats' will be taken to indicate the normal configuration. For earlier music, it may be necessary to be more precise, giving such details as the octave to which the clef refers, the total number of lines on the staff, and the exact position of accidentals: e.g. clef $d^{4/6}$, k-s *B* flat, *b* flat.

Keys and chords: either use the capital/lower-case convention (A = A major, a = A minor), or write A maj, A min (no point).

Note-values: it is often less trouble to spell these out in full. But where they are much used, and in particular for the purpose of exhibiting variant underlay, the values from long to semihemidemisemiquaver may be represented by small superscript letters as follows: l b s m c q sq sdq hdsq shdsq. A dot on the superscript line may serve to indicate a dotted note, round brackets to indicate a rest; ties may be indicated by hyphens, e.g. c-q. But any consistent method may be used. If necessary, write pitch-names below time-symbols, and the text below that.

Sigla for sources: bold-type capitals stand out clearly and are strongly recommended where the readings of two or more sources are mixed up in a single continuous commentary. But any system of abbreviation may be used provided that it does not cause confusion with other abbreviations.

All abbreviations, except for the most obvious, require prior explanation. In addition to those already given, the following are likely to be of widespread usefulness:

k-s (s)	key-signature (s)
t-s (s)	time-signature (s)
M	mensuration sign
P	proportional sign
NL	new line
LH	later hand (insertion by a subsequent scribe)

Suggested Standardized
Part-names and Abbreviations

Thirteenth to fourteenth centuries

Tenor	T	⎞ Not normally named in
Duplum *or* Motetus	Du *or* Mo	⎟ sources but derived from
Triplum	Tr	⎬ contemporary theory.
Quadruplum	Q	⎟ Use 'Motetus' only for
		⎠ texted voices.

or I, II, III, IV: order of parts as in score, *not* as suggested by above
nomenclature. In English music one may additionally find:

Tenor *or* Pes (Primus Pes)	T *or* Pes (PP)
Quartus Cantus *or* Secundus Pes	QC *or* SP

Fourteenth to fifteenth centuries

Tenor	T
Contratenor	Ct

Upper parts are not normally named in source. Supply:

Cantus *or* Discantus *or* Superius	C *or* D *or* S
Cantus Primus, Cantus Secundus, *etc.*	C1, C2, *etc.*

In 'English Descant' in three parts, where the traditionally supplied
designations have been Treble, Tenor, and Counter, the correct part-
names are more probably:

Triplex (Treble)	Tr
Medius (Mean)	M
Tenor	T

Other English voice-names, found in later fifteenth-century sources,
include:

Quatriplex (Quatreble)	Q
Contratenor (Countertenor)	Ct
Bassus (Bass)	B

(Most of these are also used in Anglican church music of later periods.)

Later Renaissance period

Cantus, Discantus, Superius	C, D, S
Cantus Primus, Cantus Secundus	C1, C2
Altus, Alto	A
Tenor, Tenore	T
Bassus, Basso	B
Quintus, Sextus, *etc.*	V, VI, *etc.*[1]
Bassus Generalis	BG

Renaissance (and early Baroque) instrumental nomenclature varies so much that no hard and fast rules can be stated. Adopt contemporary terminology where possible, and abbreviate clearly. Use arabic numerals to denote the 'first', 'second', etc., of a group of identically named parts. For keyboard music use in the commentary I, II for the two staves of the transcription.

Baroque and Classical

Most designations are Italian or Italian-derived. Use S, A, T, B for the standard voice-ranges, and arabic numerals for 'first', 'second', etc. The following list includes the commonest instrumental designations, but others indicated in the sources may be similarly treated. Original French and German terms require a comparable method.

Flauto (Flute = recorder *or* transverse flute)	Fl
Oboe	Ob
Clarinetto (Clarinet)	Cl
Fagotto (Bassoon)	Fag (Bn)
Corno (Horn)	Cor (Hn)
Tromba, Clarino (Trumpet)	Tr (Tpt)
Trombone	Tbn
Timpani (Kettledrums)	Timp (Kd)
Violino (Violin)	Vn
Viola	Va
Violoncello (Cello)	Vc
Contrabasso (Double Bass)	Cb (DB)

This last is rare in the sources. If the source has 'Basso', retain it, unabbreviated. Use also where appropriate:

Basso Continuo	BC
Cembalo (Harpsichord, Keyboard)	Cemb (Hpsd, Kbd)
Organo (Organ)	Org
Pianoforte (Piano)	Pfte

Note also the frequent need for:

Concertino	Conc
Ripieno	Rip

In general, retain original nomenclature and abbreviate intelligibly, but avoid freakish or misleading designations. The designation on the cover of a partbook may not be the most helpful one for a specific piece within (and may indeed not be contemporary). Be consistent as between score and critical commentary. In the prefatory material follow an approved method for the citation of books, articles, titles of musical works, etc.

---

[1] Roman numerals are preferable in order to avoid confusion with the usage just established for arabic. And occasionally one will need (e.g. in G. Gabrieli) such devices as X1, X2.

APPENDIX III

Sample Score-Layouts

1 Thirteenth-century motet (Mo 29/21: Montpellier, Faculté de Médecine MS H 196, ff. 44v–45r: cf. the editions of Rokseth and Tischler)

2 Fourteenth-century (Philippe de Vitry: Ivrea, Bibl. Cap., MS without shelf-mark, ff. 23v–24r). See also Ex. 1 in main text.

3 Fifteenth-century chanson (anon.: Florence, Bibl. naz. centrale, Magliabecchi XIX. 176, ff. 1v–2r). Three methods of barring: cf. Ex. 2 in main text.

(c)

Prochain de deul

Tenor

Contratenor

4 Sixteenth-century motet (Guerrero, 1555 *a 4*, no. 3). Two methods of
   barring: cf. *Monumentos de la música española*, xxxvi, no. 2 (halved
   values, bar-lines through whole score).

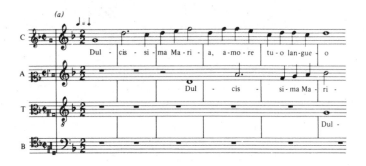

(a)

C   Dul - cis - si - ma Ma - ri - a, a - mo - re tu - o lan - gue   o

A   Dul - cis   si - ma Ma - ri -

T   Dul -

B

(b)

Dul - cis - si - ma Ma - ri - a

Dul -

5 English instrumental consort (Byrd, In Nomine: London, Brit. Lib.,
   Add. 31390, ff. 120v–121r). Other methods of barring, choice of clefs,
   and note-values are possible: cf. *The Byrd Edition*, xvii, no. 22 (G and
   F clefs, halved values, bar-lines through whole score). A specifically
   instrumental nomenclature could be substituted for the conventional,
   neutral one adopted here (the source used has none).

6 English lute song (Dowland, 1597, no. 14). Rebarred, with original shown above vocal staff and in the lute tablature. ATB vocal parts (for partsong performance) omitted. Cf. *The English Lute-Songs*, I, i–ii, no. 14, and *MB*, vi, no. 14 (partsong version in halved values).

7 Baroque trio sonata (Purcell, *Sonnata's of III Parts*, no. 1). Two methods: the abbreviated layout of 7(*b*) is suitable in many instances but the full layout of 7(*a*) is essential for some movements and it is preferable to be consistent throughout a publication. Cf. *The Works of Henry Purcell*, vol. v, and the facsimile ed. Richard Luckett (Cambridge, 1975).

8 Early Baroque polychoral work (G. Gabrieli, *Sacrae symphoniae* . . . *liber secundus*, Venice, 1615). Cf. *CMM*, XII, iv, no. 5 (using *Mensurstrich* within each choir). C clefs are retained for instrumental parts where appropriate. The division into choirs is part of the editorial task, as is the arrangement of the voices generally.

9 Early Classical symphonic work (T. A. Arne, *Four New Overtures or Symphonies*, London, 1767). Cf. *MC*, iii, in which both a string bass and a keyboard bass are provided. As the original publication has only the one part, this is unnecessary. For an example of Baroque concerto layout, see Ex. 5 in main text.

APPENDIX IV

Editorial Treatment of Accidentals

The principles involved in the editorial treatment of accidentals may be summarized as follows:

1. The edition should be in 'modern notation', i.e.

(a) any key-signature applies until changed or cancelled: its constituent accidentals apply to every octave-pitch on (or above or below) the staff on which they are placed; they should appear in standard modern configurations; 'partial' signatures (i.e. varying from staff to staff) may be retained except (normally) in keyboard music;

(b) accidentals during the course of a line apply for the (editorial) bar in which they occur unless cancelled within it. They should appear in modern form (e.g. avoiding ♮♯, replacing ♯ or ♭ by ♮ where appropriate, and printing 𝄪 for ♯ where the latter has been used to add to the effect of a sharp already in the key-signature);

(c) cancellations should appear in the form which restores the *status quo* in the key-signature.

2. The score and the commentary together should make it possible to reconstruct the incidence of accidentals in the sole or primary source at least, and in any other source of which the readings are being used. Information from more than one source, however, should not normally be conflated in the score: accidentals found only in subsidiary sources are best regarded as 'editorial' if adopted at all. The record need not embrace the exact positioning of accidentals in relation to the notes (e.g. some distance before, or above, or below) unless this gives rise to ambiguity or to the possibility that some accidentals are more authoritative than others. The fact of later addition to the source should always be recorded, whether or not such accidentals are given in the score. The following methods are recommended:

(a) the precise configuration of the original key-signature should be indicated on a preliminary staff or in the commentary unless, as in more recent sources, it is consistently identical to modern convention. All subsequent changes should be noted in the commentary, irrespective of any corresponding changes in the edition (unless these are consistently precisely identical);

(b) accidentals in the source occurring during the line are printed full-size in the ordinary way. Those which in modern notation would normally be regarded as redundant may be treated in one of three ways:

(i) they may be given in the score (editorially the most convenient method but not always acceptable in editions for wide circulation);
(ii) they may be noted in the commentary;

(iii) they may be 'negatively noted' in the commentary, i.e. their absence recorded in situations in which the scribe or printer would normally have given them (suitable when the original method is to mark all accidentals except for those inflecting immediately repeated notes, and to avoid specifying cancellations except in that context or as a precautionary measure);

(c) implied accidentals (not notated in the source) are printed small. There are three possible circumstances:

(i) to correct the difference between the modern and the original key-signature, whether this arises from changed conventions as to octave-duplication (see p. 30) or from the editor's addition or subtraction of a pitch-class. (The absence of a correcting accidental will imply that a corresponding inflection has been admitted editorially, or is present in the source but 'redundant');

(ii) to reflect the 'prolonged validity' of an accidental in the line, i.e. its inferred validity beyond the (editorial) bar in which it occurs (normally only in medieval or early Renaissance music). If such prolonged validity can be assumed, it is necessary to indicate the lineation of the source, as such validity does not normally extend beyond the end of the line in the original;

(iii) to reflect 'reduced validity', i.e. inferred cancellation within the (editorial) bar even though not noted in the source.

If (a) and (b) above are strictly adhered to, there will be no confusion as to which of these circumstances applies in any given instance.

(d) Purely editorial accidentals should be printed (small) above or below the staff (medieval and Renaissance music)[1] or in square brackets (Baroque and Classical music, also possibly in Renaissance keyboard music).

(e) Editorial cautionary accidentals, i.e. ones not strictly required by the modern notation or present in the source, should be placed before the note in round brackets.

3. In the case of finger-placement tablatures, or certain types of keyboard notation, all cancellations of accidentals in the line may be printed full-size. This is highly desirable in finger-placement tablatures, in which accidentals as such do not occur; it may also be advisable in certain forms of keyboard notation, including letter-tablatures, in which accidentals are indicated by special shapes or signs and cancelling signs are non-existent or at least very rare. For purely editorial accidentals, if needed, one of the methods given under 2(d) should be used; omissions beyond the first in any bar are dealt with as in 2(b)(iii); editorial cautionary accidentals require no special sign. Note that lute tablatures often imply a key-signature as well as accidentals in the line: keyboard notations to which the same methods apply may also have key-signatures added or supplemented. But if, in the case of keyboard music, any ambiguity results, the methods of 2 should be used in full.

4. Since no rules, however carefully drafted, can cover every possible contingency, the editor must in every case fully describe his method.

---

[1] The further differentiation of editorial accidentals notated in this way, as optional (within round brackets, or with ? attached) or essential, is also possible.

Select Bibliography

Only a small selection of the many hundreds—perhaps even thousands—of relevant works has been cited. This is particularly the case in section 1, devoted to literary studies, where the object has been to indicate the scope of the subject and the ways in which it can help the musical editor, rather than to provide even a condensed guide for musicologists in general. Some works are cited for their specific content; most, however, are given as illustrations of method or for the sake of their own more substantial bibliographies.

1. Literary

(a) Techniques of Editing[1]

Brown, Arthur: 'The Transmission of the Text', *Medieval and Renaissance Studies*, ed. John Lievesay (Durham, NC, 1968), 3–20

Dearing, Vinton: *Principles and Practice of Textual Analysis* (Berkeley, Ca., 1974)

Foulet, Alfred, and Speer, Mary: *On Editing Old French Texts* (Lawrence, Kansas, c. 1979)

Gaskell, Philip: *From Writer to Reader: Studies in Editorial Method* (Oxford, 1978)

Hill, T.: 'Spelling and the Bibliographer', *The Library*, ser. 5, xviii (1963), 1–20

Housman, A. E.: 'The Application of Thought to Textual Criticism', *Proceedings of the Classical Association*, xviii (1921), 67–84, repr. in *Art and Error: Modern Textual Editing*, ed. Ronald Gottesman and Scott Bennett (London, 1970), 1–16

Maas, Paul: *Textual Criticism* (Oxford, 1958). Transl. by Barbara Flower from *Textkritik*, 3rd edn., 1957

Medieval Manuscripts and Textual Criticism, ed. Christopher Kleinheinz (Chapel Hill, NC, 1976)

The Oxford Classical Dictionary, 2nd edn., ed. N. G. L. Hammond and H. H. Scullard (Oxford, 1970), art. 'Textual Criticism'

Reynolds, L.D., and Wilson, N.G.: *Scribes and Scholars: A Guide to the Transmission of Greek and Latin Literature* (Oxford, 1974), ch. 6, 'Textual Criticism', 186–213, and Notes, 247–50. Bibliography given there is not, for the most part, repeated here.

West, Martin: *Textual Criticism and Editorial Technique Applied to Greek and Latin Texts* (Stuttgart, 1973)

Westcott, B.F., and Hort, F.J.A. (eds.): *The New Testament in the Original Greek*, 2 vols. (Cambridge, 1881). Vol. ii, *Introduction* and *Appendix*,

---

[1] A longer list, to which I am indebted, appears in Boorman (1981), cited below s.v. 2 (c) (*i*).

contains as Part II of the *Introduction*, pp. 19–72, a penetrating and original discussion, 'The Methods of Textual Criticism'.

(b) Palaeography

Bischoff, Bernhard: *Paläographie des römischen Altertums und des abend-ländischen Mittelalters* (Berlin, 1979). Excellent bibliographies, especially in footnotes.

Cambridge Bibliography of English Literature (Cambridge, 1970), esp. art. 'Palaeography'.

Cappelli, Adriano: *(Lexicon abbreviaturarum . . .). Dizionario di abbreviature latine et italiane* (5th edn., Milan, 1954)

Hunt, Richard: 'Palaeography', *Chamber's Encyclopaedia*, x (London, 1950)

Jenkinson, Hilary: *The Later Court Hands in England, from the Fifteenth to Seventeenth Century* (Cambridge, 1927)

Lowe, E. A.: *Handwriting: Our Medieval Legacy* (2nd edn., Rome, 1969)

Lowe, E. A.: *Palaeographical Papers* (Oxford, 1972)

Parkes, M. B.: *English Cursive Book Hands 1250–1500* (2nd edn., London, 1979)

Thompson, Sir Edward Maunde: *An Introduction to Greek and Latin Palaeography* (Oxford, 1912; repr. New York, 1965)

Thomson, S. H.: *Latin Book Hands of the later Middle Ages 1100–1500* (Cambridge, 1969)

(c) Codicology and Bibliography

Bischoff, Bernhard, op. cit.

Briquet, C. M.: *Les Filigranes* (Geneva, 1907, repr. 1968 with additions)

Cambridge Bibliography of English Literature (Cambridge, 1970)

Heawood, E.: *Watermarks* (Hilversum, 1950, repr. 1969 with suppl.)

Ivy, G. S.: 'The Bibliography of the Manuscript Book', *The English Library before 1700*, ed. F. Wormald and C. E. Wright (London, 1958), 32–65

Jayne, Sears: *Library Catalogues of the English Renaissance* (Berkeley, Ca., and Los Angeles, 1956)

Ker, N. R.: *Medieval Libraries of Great Britain* (London, 1964)

Ker, N. R.: *Medieval Manuscripts in British Libraries* (Oxford, 1969–)

Medieval Learning and Literature: Essays Presented to R. W. Hunt, ed. J. J. G. Alexander and M. T. Gibson (Oxford, 1976)

Medieval Scribes, Manuscripts and Libraries: Essays Presented to N. R. Ker, ed. M. B. Parkes and A. G. Watson (London, 1978)

Robinson, P. R.: 'The "Booklet": A Self-contained Unit in Composite MSS', *Codicologica*, iii, Literae textuales (1980), 46–69.

Walther, Hans: *Initia carminum ac versuum aevi posterioris latinorum* (Göttingen, 1892 ff.; 2nd edn., Göttingen, 1969)

Watson, A. G.: *Catalogue of Dated and Dateable Manuscripts c. 700–1600 in the Department of Manuscripts, the British Library* (London, 1979)

Consult also the published catalogues of individual libraries, too numerous to mention here, and works on specific libraries of former times.

2. Musical

(a) General

(i) Editing and Interpretation

Brown, Howard Mayer: 'Editing', *The New Grove Dictionary of Music and Musicians*, 20 vols. (London, 1980). Useful bibliography, little of it duplicated here

Carapetyan, Armen: 'Problems of Editing and Publishing Old Music', *MD*, xv (1961), 5–14

Dart, Thurston: *The Interpretation of Music* (4th edn., London, 1967)

Dolmetsch, Arnold: *The Interpretation of the Music of the XVII and XVIII Centuries* (2nd edn., London, [1946])

Donington, Robert: *The Interpretation of Early Music* (3rd edn., London, 1974)

Emery, Walter: *Editions and Musicians* (London, 1957)

(ii) Notation

Apel, Willi: *The Notation of Polyphonic Music 900–1600* (5th edn., Cambridge, Mass., 1953, repr. 1961)

Rastall, Richard: *The Notation of Western Music* (London etc., 1983)

Wolf, Johannes: *Handbuch der Notationskunde*, 2 vols. (Leipzig, 1913–19, repr. Hildesheim, 1963)

Wolf, Johannes: *Musikalische Schrifttafeln* (Bückeburg and Leipzig, 1922–3)

(iii) Bibliography (including works on limited periods)

Brown, Howard Mayer: *Instrumental Music Printed before 1600: A Bibliography* (Cambridge, Mass., 1965)

Census-Catalogue of Manuscript Sources of Polyphonic Music 1400–1550 (Neuhausen-Stuttgart, 1979–)

Daniel, Ralph T., and Le Huray, Peter: *The Sources of English Church Music 1549–1660* (London, 1972)

Eitner, Robert: *Biographisch-bibliographisches Quellen-Lexicon*, 10 vols. (Leipzig, 1900–04; Supplement, 4 vols., 1912–16; repr. 1947; 2nd rev. edn., 1959–60)

Eitner, Robert, with C. F. Pohl, A. Lagenberg and F. X. Haberl: *Bibliographie der Musik-Sammelwerke des XVI und XVII Jahrhunderts* (Berlin, 1877; repr. 1963)

Heartz, Daniel: *Pierre Attaingnant, Royal Printer of Music* (Berkeley, Ca. and Los Angeles, 1969)

Hopkinson, Cecil: *A Dictionary of Parisian Music Publishers, 1701–1950* (London, 1954)

Humphries, Charles and Smith, William C.: *Music Publishing in the British Isles* (London, 1953)

King, A. Hyatt: *Four Hundred Years of Music Printing* (London, 1964)

LaRue, Jan: 'Watermarks and Musicology', *AcM*, xxxiii (1961), 120–46. With extensive annotated bibliography

LaRue, Jan, with J. S. G. Simmons: 'Watermarks', *The New Grove Dictionary*. Useful short bibliography

Meyer (afterwards Meyer-Baer), Kathi: 'The Printing of Music 1473-1934', *The Dolphin*, ii (New York, 1935), 171-207

Meyer (afterwards Meyer-Baer), Kathi: *Liturgical Music Incunabula: A Descriptive Catalogue* (London, 1962)

Pattison, Bruce: 'Notes on Early Music Printing', *The Library*, IV/xix (1939), 389-421

Répertoire International des Sources Musicales [*RISM*] (Munich and Duisburg, 1960-)

Sartori, Claudio: *Bibliografia della musica strumentale italiana stampata in Italia fino al 1700*, 2 vols. (Florence, 1952-68)

Sartori, Claudio: *Bibliografia delle opere musicale stampati da Ottaviano Petrucci* (Florence, 1948)

Sartori, Claudio: *Dizionario degli editori musicali italiani* (Florence, 1958)

Schnapper, Edith B.: *The British-Union Catalogue of Early Music* [*BUCEM*], 2 vols. (London, 1957)

Smith, William C.: *A Bibliography of the Musical Works Published by John Walsh during the Years 1695-1720* (London and New York, 1948)

Smith, William C., and Humphries, Charles: *A Bibliography... John Walsh ... 1721-1766* (London, 1968)

Smith, William C., and Humphries, Charles: *Handel: A Descriptive Catalogue of the Early Editions* (2nd edn., London, 1970)

Steele, Robert: *The Earliest English Music Printing* (London, 1903)

Tyson, Alan: *The Authentic English Editions of Beethoven* (London, 1963)

Consult also individual library catalogues, composer-catalogues and relevant articles in *MGG* and *The New Grove*.

(b) Medieval

(i) Editing

Apel, Willi: 'The Partial Signatures in the Sources up to 1450', *AcM*, x (1938), 1-13

Dömling, Wolfgang: 'Zur Überlieferung der Musikalischen Werke Guillaume de Machauts', *Die Musikforschung*, xxii (1969), 189-95

Hoppin, Richard H.: 'Partial Signatures and Musica Ficta in Some Early 15th-Century Sources', *JAMS*, vi (1953), 197-215

Hughes, David: 'The Sources of Christus Manens', *Aspects of Medieval and Renaissance Music*, ed. Jan LaRue and others (London, 1967), 423-34.

Lowinsky, Edward E.: 'The Function of Conflicting Signatures in Early Polyphonic Music', *MQ*, xxxi (1945), 227-60

Planchart, Alejandro Enrique: 'The Transmission of Medieval Chant', *Music in Medieval and Early Modern Europe*, ed. Iain Fenlon (Cambridge, 1981), 347-63

Roesner, Edward H.: 'The Problem of Chronology in the Transmission of Organum Duplum', ibid., 365-99

Van der Werf, Hendrik: *The Chansons of the Troubadours and Trouvères* (Utrecht, 1972)

For *musica ficta* see also Chap. 2, note 15.

(ii) Notation

Parrish, Carl: *The Notation of Medieval Music* (New York, 1957)

Suñol, G.: *Introduction à la paléographie musicale grégorienne* (Paris, 1935)

Wagner, Peter: *Neumenkunde* (= vol. ii of *Einführung in die gregorianischen Melodien*; 2nd edn., Leipzig, 1912, repr. Hildesheim, 1962)

Waite, William: *The Rhythm of Twelfth-Century Polyphony* (New Haven and London, 1954)

Wolf, Johannes: *Geschichte der Mensuralnotation von 1250-1460*, 3 vols. (Leipzig, 1904, repr. in 1 vol., Hildesheim, 1963)

For English notational practice, consult especially the introduction to *EECM*, xxvi.

(iii) Editions

Plainsong has rarely been satisfactorily edited. Apart from facsimiles, those which approach nearest to preserving the essentials in some form of modernized notation are those of Stäblein in *MMMA*. Much the same may be said of song, except for diplomatic transcriptions, though J. Beck (*Le Chansonnier Cangé*, 1927, and, with L. Beck, *Le Manuscrit du roi*, 1938) made a brave attempt in the context of modal theory. The subsequent editions of Gennrich have been less satisfactory, though philologically and bibliographically very well documented. Van der Werf (op. cit.) offers a well-edited selection, while his corpus of trouvère melodies, published in *MMMA*, xi–xii, though definitive as far as it goes, is far from complete, lacking full verbal texts and offering no clues to interpretation. Amongst older editions of polyphonic music, those of Wagner (*Die Gesänge der Jakobusliturgie*, Freiburg, 1931), Husmann (*Die drei- und vierstimmige Notre-Dame-Organa*, Leipzig, 1940, repr. 1967), Aubry (*Cent Motets du XIIIe siècle*, Paris, 1908, repr. 1964), Rokseth (*Polyphonies du XIIIe siècle*, Paris, 1935-9) and Ludwig (*Guillaume de Machaut, Musikalische Werke*, Leipzig, 1926-9) are amongst the most thorough, though their methods are in some respects outdated. The St. Martial repertory has never been fully edited on scholarly principles. Since Husmann, valuable editions of Notre Dame music by Waite (op. cit.), G. A. Anderson (*The Latin Compositions in Fascicules VII and VIII of the Notre Dame Manuscript Wolfenbüttel Helmstadt, 1099*, 2 vols., New York, 1976) and E. Thurston (*The Works of Perotin*, New York, 1970) have appeared. Recent editions of the Bamberg MS (ed. G. A. Anderson, *CMM*, LXXV) and Montpellier MS (ed. H. Tischler, Madison, 1978) are a refinement on those of Aubry and Rokseth respectively, though they lack the facsimiles and extended commentaries of the latter. In the fourteenth century, the highest scholarly standards are upheld in the series *CMM* and *PMFC*. The recent *Oxford Anthology of Music: Medieval Music*, ed. T. Marrocco and N. Sandon (London, 1977), and the anthology with Richard Hoppin's *Medieval Music* (New York, 1978) are both excellently done and cover a wide variety of material. See also Chap. 2, note 3.

(c) Renaissance

(i) Editing and Bibliography

Atlas, Alan W.: 'Conflicting Attributions in Italian Sources of the Nether-
landish Chanson, *c.* 1465–*c.* 1505: A Progress Report on a New Hypo-
thesis', *Music in Medieval and Early Modern Europe*, ed. Iain Fenlon
(Cambridge, 1981), 249–93

Bent, Margaret: 'Some Criteria for Establishing Relationships between
Sources of Late-Medieval Polyphony', ibid., 295–317

Boorman, Stanley: 'Limitations and Extensions of Filiation Technique',
ibid., 319–46; q.v. for much additional bibliography

Clulow, Peter: 'Publication Dates for Byrd's Latin Masses', *ML*, xlvii
(1966), 1–9. A classic study of the uses of typographical evidence.

Mendel, Arthur, and others: 'Problems in Editing the Music of Josquin des
Prez: A Critique of the First Edition and Proposals for the Second
Edition', *Josquin des Prez*, ed. E. E. Lowinsky (London, 1976), 723–54.
This is an authoritative discussion of many of the problems encoun-
tered, while pp. 179–293 of this useful volume are devoted to studies of
the sources of Josquin's music.

(ii) Notation

Consult the items listed above under 2(a)(*ii*). In addition, for a useful insight into many aspects of fifteenth-century mensuration:

Hamm, Charles: *A Chronology of the Works of Guillaume Dufay, Based
on a Study of Mensural Practice* (Princeton, 1964)

(iii) Editions

The series *CMM*, *EECM* and *MB* between them offer a generally high
standard of editing, as does *RRMR* in a more modest way; *MRM* offers
something far more substantial in the way of commentary, even to the
extent of the tail wagging the dog. Amongst older editions of individual
composers, those of Obrecht (Wolf), Ockeghem (Plamenac), and Josquin
(Smijers) were outstanding in their thoroughness. This tradition and its
standards are maintained in such series as *Musikalische Denkmäler* (see esp.
vols. vii and viii, devoted to Masses by Isaac, ed. M. Staehelin) and *Das
Erbe deutscher Musik*. *The Byrd Edition*, ed. Philip Brett (London, 1970–)
has established sound methods. The long-established *Das Chorwerk*, ed.
F. Blume and K. Gudewill, combines scholarly probity with practical
usefulness, as does the more recently founded *Mapa Mundi*, under the
direction of Bruno Turner. The *Oxenford Imprint*, ed. David Wulstan,
is distinguished by a high standard of presentation and a thoughtful
approach to the problems of editing the English choral repertory.

(d) Baroque and Classical: Editing and Interpretation

Arnold, F.T.: *The Art of Accompaniment from a Thorough-Bass* (London,
1931)

Donington, Robert: *A Performer's Guide to Baroque Music* (London, 1973)

Larsen, J. P.: *Die Haydn-Überlieferung* (Copenhagen, 1939)

Mies, P.: *Textkritische Untersuchungen bei Beethoven* (Munich and Duisburg, 1957)

See also much of the material listed under 2(a)(*iii*), and the modern collected editions of Bach, Haydn, Mozart, Beethoven, Schubert, Berlioz, etc. Many of the more popular collections, such as *Hortus musicus* (Bärenreiter), *Diletto musicale* (Doblinger, Vienna), *Le Pupitre* (Heugel, Paris), *Musica da Camera* (OUP, London), and Nagel's *Musik Archiv*, offer a generally acceptable standard in a format designed to appeal to the non-scholarly user.

(e)   Preparation of Copy

(i)   General, Literary

Hart's Rules for Compositors and Readers (39th edn., Oxford and New York, 1983)

The Oxford Dictionary for Writers and Editors (Oxford, 1981)

(ii)   Musical

Boustead, Alan: *Writing Down Music* (London, 1975). Though not primarily concerned with the preparation of copy, it contains much useful advice.

Donato, A.: *Preparing Music Manuscript* (Englewood Cliffs, NJ, 1963)

Index

1. COMPOSERS, THEORISTS, AND THEIR WORKS

scoring, for voices, 7, 10
sesquialtera, 21n, 26 (Table V), 47
sigla, *see under* abbreviations
Silbenstrich, 37
slurs:
    editorial, 11, 12, 35, 103
    original, 72, 88, 91
small print, use of, 93, 94, 95, 103
    see also under accidentals
sources, 4, 5, 112
    discussion of, 6–7
    treatment of, in commentary, 9,
        93–4
spelling, 41–2, 62–3, 92
    in editorial letterpress, 100
staccato, 88
staff, staves:
    preliminary, 10, 32, 50, 53
    small, 84
    subsidiary, 7, 88
stems, direction of, 89
    see also under beaming
stemma, stemmatic method, 4, 5
strumming effects, 91
style brisé, 91
syllables:
    notational treatment of, 12, 34,
        42–3, 71–2, 92, 96–7
    placing of, 96
    separation of (i.e. word-division),
        42, 64, 92, 96
    see also under *Silbenstrich*
syncopation, 25

tablature:
    keyboard, 60, 65, 67 (Table VI),
        90, 113
    lute (and other finger-placement
        systems), 60, 66–8, 91, 113
tactus, theory of, 27, 28, 46, 48, 49
tempo markings, 99
    editorial, 11, 71
    original, 71
tempo relationships, 11, 69, 71
tenor (in motets, etc.), *see under*
    cantus firmi

text, musical:
    establishment of, 10n
    synoptic presentation of, 94
text, verbal:
    presentation of, 41–4, 62–4, 96–7,
        103
    translation of, 43
    see also under punctuation, spelling,
        syllables, underlay
textual criticism, 5
ties, editorial, 11, 61, 103
time-signatures:
    editorial, 49–50, 71, 99
    original, 70–1
time-values, *see under* note-values
titles, *see under* headings and titles
transcription into modern notation, 1–2,
    13, 32
transposition:
    editorial, 29, 54–5
    in earlier times, 54n
    in instrumental parts, 73, 91–2
trio sonatas, 85, 109–10 (Ex.)
tripla, 21n, 26 (Table V), 47
triple time, editorial treatment of,
    46–8, 69
tunings, special, 91

underlay, verbal, 9, 43–4, 63–4

variation movements, omitted bass
    lines in, 91
variants, *see under* errors and variants
virga, 61
'vocal' scores, 93

Winchester Troper, *see under* Manu-
    scripts: Cambridge, Corpus Chrisi
    College, MS 473
word-division, *see under* syllables,
    separation of
word-underlay, *see under* underlay,
    verbal